CAMPAIGN • 198

THE SAMURAI INVASION OF KOREA 1592–98

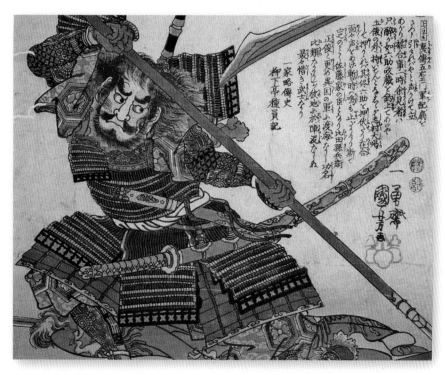

STEPHEN TURNBULL

ILLUSTRATED BY PETER DENNIS

Series editors Marcus Cowper and Nikolai Bogdanovic

First published in Great Britain in 2008 by Osprey Publishing,
Midland House, West Way, Botley, Oxford OX2 0PH, UK
443 Park Avenue South, New York, NY 10016, USA
E-mail: info@ospreypublishing.com

A CIP catalogue record for this book is available from the British Library.

ISBN: 978 1 84603 254 7

Editorial by Ilios Publishing Ltd, Oxford, UK (www.iliospublishing.com)
Page layout by: The Black Spot
Index by Alan Thatcher
Typeset in Myriad Pro and Sabon
Maps by The Map Studio Ltd
3D bird's-eye views by The Black Spot
Battlescene illustrations by Peter Dennis
Originated by PDQ Digital Media Solutions
Printed in China through Worldprint Ltd.

08 09 10 11 12   10 9 8 7 6 5 4 3 2 1

FOR A CATALOGUE OF ALL BOOKS PUBLISHED BY OSPREY MILITARY
AND AVIATION PLEASE CONTACT:

NORTH AMERICA
Osprey Direct, c/o Random House Distribution Center, 400 Hahn Road,
Westminster, MD 21157
E-mail: info@ospreydirect.com

ALL OTHER REGIONS
Osprey Direct UK, P.O. Box 140 Wellingborough, Northants, NN8 2FA, UK
E-mail: info@ospreydirect.co.uk

www.ospreypublishing.com

DEDICATION

To Richard and Helen on the occasion of their wedding, 23 August 2008.

PREFACE AND ACKNOWLEDGEMENTS

The Japanese invasion of Korea in 1592 and the subsequent six-year-long
war between China and Japan was one of the most important and tragic
events in pre-modern East Asian history. It gave the region its first
'world war', and caused a degree of devastation in Korea itself that was
unmatched until the Korean War of the 1950s. It has also been a story that
has for too long been told from only one point of view. Japan's occupation
of Korea during the 20th century and a lack of access to Chinese source
materials have meant that this has been a conflict where the history
was very much written by the aggressors. At the hands of historians
influenced by the Japanese nationalism of the 1930s, Chinese and Korean
victories were dismissed, fighting retreats were exaggerated into major
achievements, and atrocities were airbrushed out of the record. My
previous work *Samurai Invasion: Japan's Korean War 1592–98* (Cassells:,
London, 2002) suffered in particular from the lack of a Chinese perspective,
but in this book, as in my recent *Japanese Castles in Korea* (Osprey
Publishing Ltd: Oxford, 2007), number 67 in the Osprey Fortress series,
I have had access to material that has allowed a more balanced view
of this very important campaign.

In this work I have expressed Korean names using the older style of Korean
Romanization rather than the new style that appears in Fortress 67:
Japanese Castles in Korea. This is because much of the action of the
Japanese invasions took place in what is now North Korea, where
the old style is still used. It is also preferable for people's names and is
therefore consistent with most academic writing on the subject. I wish to
acknowledge the help received from the War Memorial Museum in Seoul,
the Nagoya Castle Museum in Kyūshū and the helpful comments by
Kenneth Swope, whose recent research into Chinese sources for the Korean
invasions have added greatly to my understanding of the conflict. Recent
visits to Korea, Japan and China have also enabled me to illustrate the
present book with many new pictures.

EDITOR'S NOTE

Unless otherwise indicated, all images in this book are the property
of the author.

ARTIST'S NOTE

Readers may care to note that the original paintings from which the colour
plates in this book were prepared are available for private sale. The
Publishers retain all reproduction copyright whatsoever. All enquiries
should be addressed to:

Peter Dennis, The Park, Mansfield, Notts, NG18 2AT, UK

The Publishers regret that they can enter into no correspondence upon
this matter.

THE WOODLAND TRUST

Osprey Publishing are supporting the Woodland Trust, the UK's leading
woodland conservation charity, by funding the dedication of trees

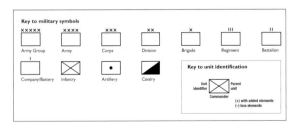

CONTENTS

THE STRATEGIC SITUATION

Even though the invasion of Korea was an act of unprovoked aggression by Japan against its immediate neighbour, the campaign has to be seen in the context of the overall strategic situation that existed in East Asia during the last quarter of the 16th century. It was a position dominated by China and its great empire of the Ming dynasty, whose pre-eminence was threatened in 1592 by a small island neighbour that had been obsessed with its own internal wars for over a hundred years. On previous occasions the lawless state of Japan had affected China in the form of pirate raids, but it was the very fact of Japanese disunity that had led it to pose no major threat to the stability of the Ming. This situation was to change radically in 1591, when Japan became reunited under one sword.

The reunification of Japan was achieved by Toyotomi Hideyoshi (1532–98). After a long military campaign that had reached from one end of Japan to another, Hideyoshi had brought to a close the century of sporadic civil war that historians have dubbed the *Sengoku Jidai* (The Age of Warring States), a term used by analogy with the period of that name in ancient Chinese history. It may therefore appear somewhat surprising that within one year

OPPOSITE
Kido Norishige performed an unusual feat during the capture of Seoul in 1592. The city gates were securely locked, so Norishige fastened several gun barrels together to make a stout lever and prised open the grille that was covering a water gate.

RIGHT
Admiral Yi Sunsin, the greatest hero of the defeat of the samurai invasion of Korea, is shown here discussing his plans for the battle of Okp'o, Korea's first victory over the invaders as shown on this modern painting in the Okp'o Memorial Museum on Kōje Island, South Korea.

Konishi Yukinaga, who played a prominent role throughout the campaign, leads a Japanese attack on Ming soldiers. From *Ehon Taikōki*, an illustrated life of Hideyoshi.

of having achieved peace at home, the undisputed ruler of Japan should immediately seek war overseas; particularly when one considers that the Korean invasion remains the only major act of aggression by Japan against a neighbouring country within one thousand years of its history.

Yet the Korean expedition did not come from nowhere, and the most important trigger to action was Hideyoshi's own grandiose dream of overseas military conquest. There is considerable evidence that he had been planning such a move for several years as the logical extension of his unstoppable triumphs at home. When Hideyoshi received Father Gaspar Coelho, the vice-principal of the Jesuit mission in Japan, in 1585, he disclosed to him his plans for overseas expansion and asked for two Portuguese ships to be made available, a request that was politely refused. Two years later, while setting off on the Kyūshū campaign, Hideyoshi told his companions of his intention to 'slash his way' into Korea and China. In fact his personal ambitions went further than Korea and China, and included the conquest of Taiwan, the Philippines and even India.

Hideyoshi's expectation that an international act of aggression would be an unqualified success was fully in keeping with his experience of domestic Japanese warfare over the past two decades. As his power grew he would request rival *daimyō* (warlords) to pay homage to him and accept vassal status. If they refused they were attacked by Hideyoshi's increasingly professional army. Hideyoshi was a generous victor, so that mass acts of suicide or battles to the death were rare events during his campaigns, and upon their submission the defeated *daimyō* were usually acknowledged in their existing possessions on agreeing to accept the status that they had once so unwisely declined. To treat Korea and even China in this way could well have seemed a natural progression for a successful general who had demonstrated, among his other accomplishments, the ability to move large numbers of soldiers over large distances, including across the sea. The Japanese army was well equipped and battle hardened, so to take on Korea and even Ming China with its vast resources theoretically available to oppose him, was not such a big gamble.

From a wider political perspective Hideyoshi's desire to make Korea and China into his vassal states may have been presumptive, but it was fully in the context of the way that international relations had long been handled from the Chinese side. To make China a vassal state of a neighbouring country would simply reverse the position that had existed for centuries, whereby China regarded itself as the centre of the world with its neighbours as its children. To the Ming emperors this dependent relationship was the basis of international trade and harmony. China was a universal and benevolent empire whose sovereignty had to be acknowledged by its less fortunate barbarian neighbours before the benefits of commerce could be bestowed. These supplicant barbarians must first pay homage to the Chinese emperor, who would then graciously bestow upon them titles and privileges such as being acknowledged by China as rulers of their own countries. In deep gratitude they would then bring tribute to his feet, and gifts would be showered upon them in return.

This exchange of tribute for gifts contained the essence of trade, and fruitful commercial transactions flowed from it, so most trading missions to China played along with the bizarre pantomime. Japan had always tended to be an exception to the rule, although, according to the first Ming emperor, the Japanese had entered into such a tributary relationship as early as the Han dynasty (202 BC to AD 220). In more recent memory the shogun Ashikaga Yoshimitsu (1358–1408) had indeed formally accepted vassal status and tribute trade had flourished, but with the collapse of the shogun's authority during the Age of Warring States any kowtowing by Japan to China in this way had long ceased. Sino-Japanese relations were now characterized by an aggressive attitude towards international trading rights that was manifested through the depredations of the *wakō* (Japanese pirates). In spite of their name many *wakō*, and some of their most notorious leaders, were actually Chinese, who

The horrors inflicted by the Japanese during the invasion of Korea brought back memories of the dark days of the *wakō* raids, as shown on this modern painting in the Okp'o Memorial Museum on Kŏje Island, South Korea.

organized devastating raids against China and Korea from the 1540s onwards. In response the Ming had severed both trade and tribute with Japan, but as these independent-minded buccaneers lived outside the frame of Japanese legality anyway it was a slur that worried none of them. Some of their raids were so huge that they amounted to mini-invasions of China. Thousands of *wakō* would set up temporary headquarters in places like the Zhoushan archipelago off Ningbo, where they commandeered ships and horses and struck deeply into Chinese territory to rape and pillage with impunity.

Korea too had felt the brunt of the pirates. There was a *wakō* raid on Korea in 1544, and then in 1555 a much bigger operation was launched. In a chilling precedent for what was to come, Korean resistance all but collapsed. Left waiting for their commander to arrive from Seoul, the Korean troops gave in as soon as the Japanese advanced, and by the time the general arrived he had no army to lead – only runaway soldiers hiding in the forests and no one left in reserve.

The 1555 raid was almost a dress rehearsal for the officially sanctioned overseas expedition that was to hit Korea in 1592. It was launched to a background of ignorance on Hideyoshi's part concerning the relationship between China and Korea and the likelihood that Korea would allow the Japanese army free passage to attack the Ming. Whereas Hideyoshi intended to turn the tribute system on its head by making himself ruler of China, successive kings of Korea had accepted their lowly tributary status willingly and loyally. As a result, when Korea was attacked by the nation whose outrageous behaviour had brought about the unthinkable insult of having its tribute status withdrawn, the Ming rushed to the defence of its faithful vassal. There may have been an element of self-interest in the Chinese response (a matter often exaggerated by an earlier generation of Japanese historians), but it was entirely selfless in its execution, and involved a huge commitment of resources and lives.

China also played a major role behind the scenes in the strategic build-up to the Japanese invasion. Because the depredations of the *wakō* were such a recent memory the Ming were acutely aware of Japan's military strength and possible aggressive intentions, so as soon as there was evidence that Japan was planning an officially sanctioned invasion of the East Asian mainland they hurried to warn the Koreans. For purely logistical reasons any major invasion of China had to pass through Korea because the Japanese islands of Iki and Tsushima made the sea journey comparatively easy. When free passage for Japanese troops through Korea was refused a war against Korea as a preliminary stage of a war against China became inevitable.

According to the annals of the Ming dynasty it was also believed that the Japanese advance through Korea would coincide with *wakō*-like raids against Zhejiang and Fujian provinces in China. The likelihood of such a strategy explains why the first foreign monarch to hear of Hideyoshi's plans was the king of Ryūkyū, the independent

Kuroda Nagamasa, commander of the Third Division, attacks the gate of the fortress of Hwangsŏksan during the second invasion of Korea in 1597.

archipelago between Japan and Taiwan that is now part of Japan and is known by the name of Okinawa. The 'southern route' from Japan to China passes along the Ryūkyū islands, and Hideyoshi was concerned that the Ryūkyūans, who conducted active trade with China, might alert the Ming about his plans, so in 1589 he ordered Shō Nei, the new king of Ryūkyū, to suspend all trade missions forthwith. The king refused to do this, and in fact reported the matter to a group of Chinese envoys who were about to return home, urging them to inform their emperor.

Another early warning of the invasion came to the ears of the Ming in 1591 from a Chinese trader who was captured by the Japanese. He managed to send a message back to Zhejiang saying that 100,000 Japanese troops were being massed to invade during the following year. This was very valuable intelligence, so the Wanli Emperor (r. 1573–1620) ordered that Chinese coastal defences should be strengthened. Representatives from Liaodong, the peninsula in northern China that would have been first to be attacked once Korea had fallen, sent word to the Korean king as soon as the news was conveyed to them. The Koreans certainly took the warnings seriously, and within two months a request for help from China was received at the Ming court. Its tone was optimistic with regard to the Chinese military capability, when it stated, that 'When the celestial empire comes through the mountains with its great cannon, its mighty generals, heavenly firearms and fierce troops shaking the ground, even a million Japanese troops will not be enough to stop them.'

While the invasion fleet gathered, therefore, neither the Koreans nor the Chinese were in any doubt over what Hideyoshi was planning. It is also clear that the Koreans realized that they did not have the resources to prevent a landing or drive the Japanese back into the sea. Only the Ming could do that, and as Korea's 'elder brothers' they were firmly committed to the task, so even before the first Japanese samurai had landed in Korea the strategic situation meant that three nations were prepared for war.

Korean defences were characterized by low stone walls, as shown on this modern painting in the Memorial Museum at Ŭiryŏng. They were very vulnerable to the massed harquebus fire of the Japanese.

CHRONOLOGY

The first invasion, 1592–93

1592

23 May	First Division leaves Tsushima
24 May	Fall of Pusan and death of Chŏng Pal
25 May	Capture of Tongnae
31 May	Second Division captures Kyŏngju
10 June	Japanese army reaches Seoul
16 June	First day of the naval battle of Okp'o
6 July	The Japanese army finally crosses the Imjin River
8 July	Battle of Sach'ŏn; turtle ships in action
10 July	Battle of Tangp'o
13 July	Battle of Tanghangp'o
24 July	Japanese capture P'yŏngyang
14 August	Battle of Hansando
16 August	Battle of Angolp'o
23 August	First Chinese attack on P'yŏngyang fails
24 August	Katō Kiyomasa wins the battle of Sŏngjin
6 September	Korean irregular forces recapture Ch'ŏngju
22 September	Korean monk and volunteer army are defeated at Kŭmsan
12 October	Pacification of north-east is completed by Katō Kiyomasa
12 November	First siege of Chinju

1593

5 February	Siege of P'yŏngyang begins
19 February	The retreating Japanese army enters Seoul
27 February	Battle of Pyŏkjeyek
14 March	Battle of Haengju
19 May	Liberation of Seoul by Chinese army
25 July	Second siege of Chinju

The second invasion, 1597–98

1597

24 September	Japanese attack Namwŏn
26 September	Namwŏn captured
27 September	Fall of Hwangsŏksan
17 October	Battle of Chiksan
26 October	Yi Sunsin wins the battle of Myŏngyang

1598

29 January	Siege of Ulsan begins
8 February	Ulsan is relieved
18 September	Toyotomi Hideyoshi dies
30 October	Battle of Sach'ŏn begins; battle of Sunch'ŏn begins
17 December	Battle of Noryang; death of Admiral Yi
21 December	Evacuation of Pusan begins

OPPOSING PLANS

JAPAN

Toyotomi Hideyoshi's strategic plans of campaign were based on certain assumptions drawn from what he had learned from the limited overseas expeditions carried out by the *wakō* on China. The first envisaged the submission of the Korean king either by negotiation or warfare, just as his domestic rivals had done, with no involvement from China. Hideyoshi's plans also dismissed the possibility of any intervention by the Korean navy. The invasion would therefore begin with an unopposed landing and a blitzkrieg attack that would take Seoul within days. With the Korean army as his allies and the Korean people to feed his army, massive reinforcements could be shipped over to the peninsula. There would then be an assault across the Yalu River, a march round the coast, through the Great Wall and on to Beijing.

Yet all these assumptions were flawed. The experience of the earlier raids had certainly indicated that pirates based in Japan had once acted with impunity, but that impression was long out of date, because by the end of the

Toyotomi Hideyoshi, who is regarded as the Japanese equivalent of Napoleon Bonaparte, was an accomplished general who inspired fierce loyalty in his followers and finally achieved the reunification of Japan. The invasion of Korea was his last campaign and his only failure. This painting of him in armour hangs in the Hōsei Nikō Kenshōkan in Nakamura Park, Nagoya.

Japan, China and Korea in 1592

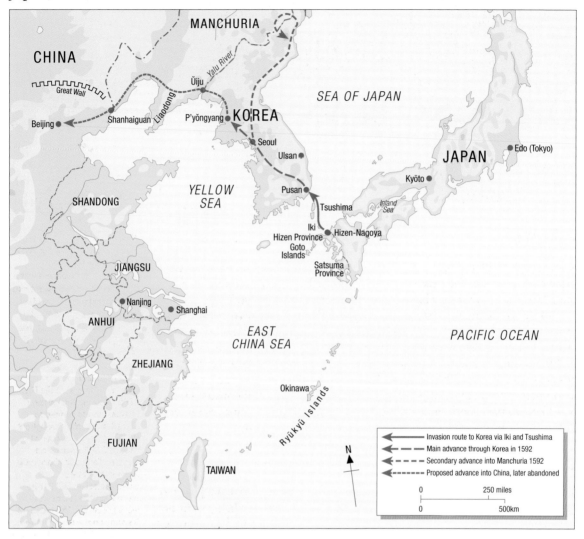

1560s the *wakō* were being regularly defeated by Chinese generals. The Korean navy had also destroyed Japanese pirate ships owing to its superiority with cannon. Nor did Hideyoshi appreciate the tributary relationship between China and Korea. Instead his ignorance of the position was so great that he seems to have believed that Korea was in some way under the control of the *daimyō* of Tsushima. As events turned out, however, Hideyoshi's strategic assumptions would prove to be correct in the short term and disastrously wrong in the long term. There was indeed a rapid collapse of Korean resistance, but this was to be followed by Korean naval victories and a decisive Chinese intervention.

At a tactical level Hideyoshi's battle plans were less fanciful but much more limited in their time scale. The landings were planned to take place in three major phases around Pusan, but any direction after the initial landings grew progressively more vague as the armies were directed northwards. Seoul was of course the primary target, so Hideyoshi envisaged the three armies converging for an attack, but beyond Seoul the plans of attack seemed to evaporate completely, a lack of direction that was to be realized on the ground.

KOREA

Korea's lack of planning for the invasion was partly responsible for the early Japanese successes. The *wakō* raid of 1555 may have been an awful memory, but all the lessons that may have been learned from it were lost. There was still a centralized command system that operated from Seoul with troops being raised locally and moved to the scene of trouble as quickly as possible. Korea's great strength in defensive preparations lay with its formidable navy, which had the resources and the firepower to locate the Japanese invasion fleet and possibly destroy it even before it left Tsushima. But Korea's navy suffered from incompetent commanders in the sea areas through which the invasion fleet was likely to pass. Both failed to see the fleet, and when the Japanese entered Pusan Harbour one ran away and the other scuttled his ships.

CHINA

The Chinese plans were always to cross the Yalu River and drive the Japanese back into the sea, but unfortunately the Korean request for help could not have come at a worse time for the Chinese. A serious mutiny had occurred in Ningxia in the north-west of China, and troops who would normally have been garrisoning the Liaodong Peninsula, and thus could have made an immediate response to a Japanese invasion of Korea, were many hundreds of kilometres away. Li Rusong, the general who was eventually to recapture P'yŏngyang, was actively fighting in Ningxia while the Japanese swept through Korea, and it was early 1593 before the Chinese were able to put their plans into action on an appropriate scale.

ABOVE LEFT
The *wajō* (Japan's coastal forts) provided the last line of defence for the Japanese when their second invasion went into reverse. This scene from *Ehon Taikōki*, an illustrated life of Hideyoshi shows perfectly the strong but temporary nature of the *wajō*.

ABOVE RIGHT
Konishi Yukinaga led the First Division during the invasion of Korea and continued to play a leading role throughout the war. It was Yukinaga who captured P'yŏngyang and was then forced to abandon it when the Chinese counterattacked. In 1597 he was almost the last general to leave Korea. This illustration of his army on the march is taken from *Ehon Taikōki*, an illustrated life of Hideyoshi.

OPPOSING COMMANDERS

JAPAN

Toyotomi Hideyoshi

Throughout the entire course of the war Toyotomi Hideyoshi never set foot in Korea, and instead left the full control of operations to the generals he trusted so well. In a tactical sense, therefore, Hideyoshi cannot be considered as one of the commanders, but, as his will drove the whole project along until he died, his political influence cannot be underestimated.

Contemporary observers note his small, wizened stature and the total lack of noble features on his monkey-like head, yet as his power grew Hideyoshi took on aristocratic trappings on a grander scale than any ruler before him. This was in marked contrast to his humble beginnings, because his father had been a peasant farmer who had served as an *ashigaru* (footsoldier) until a bullet wound invalided him out. Hideyoshi, then called Tokichirō, followed in his father's footsteps and served the *daimyō* Oda Nobunaga (1534–82) as the latter grew to become the first of Japan's great unifiers. Nobunaga had an eye for talent, and rewarded Tokichirō's successive military accomplishments by rapid promotion until, by the time of Nobunaga's murder in 1582, Hideyoshi was his most loyal general. He then became Nobunaga's avenger, and the kudos associated with this fact gave Hideyoshi the opportunity to fill the power vacuum that Nobunaga's death had left. During the next two years Hideyoshi was to challenge and defeat all other rivals, including Nobunaga's surviving sons, in a series of brilliant military campaigns. By 1585 Hideyoshi was able to begin extending the boundaries of Nobunaga's former conquests, taking in the island of Shikoku and the provinces of western Japan. The Shikoku campaign involved a successful sea crossing, and in 1587 Hideyoshi conquered the great southern Japanese island of Kyūshū in a huge and well-coordinated campaign that was to provide a model for the Korean expedition. The defeat of the Hōjō in 1590, which involved mobilizing the largest army ever seen in Japan, led to most of the northern *daimyō* submitting without a fight.

Konishi Yukinaga

Konishi Yukinaga (1558–1600), whom Hideyoshi chose to lead the invasion in 1592, was the *daimyō* of Uto in southern Higo province in Kyūshū. His unfortunate later life, which involved choosing the wrong side before the battle of Sekigahara and being executed after it, has robbed posterity of any portrait of him or any mementoes of his earlier, glorious career. It had been his political talents rather than his military skills that had first brought Konishi to

Known to the Koreans as the 'devil general', Katō Kiyomasa commanded the Second Division of the Japanese army. Following the fall of Seoul Kiyomasa pacified the north-east of Korea and made a brief incursion into Manchuria. He was to earn great glory at the siege of Ulsan in 1598. From *Ehon Taikōki*, an illustrated life of Hideyoshi.

Hideyoshi's attention when he had been employed by his master Ukita Naoie in negotiating the bloodless surrender of the Ukita domains to Hideyoshi. Loyal service during the Kyūshū campaign earned him the fief of Uto. He was baptized in 1583, and is known in the Jesuit accounts as Dom Agostinho (Augustin). Konishi Yukinaga's presence dominated the whole of the Korean expedition. He was the first commander to land and the last to leave.

Katō Kiyomasa

Katō Kiyomasa, who led the Second Division of the Japanese army, was born in the village of Nakamura, which has long since been swallowed up within the modern city of Nagoya. He was called Toranosuke (the young tiger) in his childhood, and was the son of a blacksmith who died when the boy was three years old. Because of a familial relationship between the two boys' mothers, Toyotomi Hideyoshi took Toranosuke under his wing when his father died.

Katō Kiyomasa soon proved to have a considerable aptitude for the military life, and the first opportunity to demonstrate it came at the age of 21 with the battle of Shizugatake, where the absence of a flat battlefield and lines of harquebus troops allowed the individual samurai spirit to be expressed in an unfettered way. Katō Kiyomasa fought from horseback in classic style with the support of a loyal band of samurai attendants, and wielded his favourite cross-bladed spear to great effect. It was not long before a number of enemy heads had fallen to Kiyomasa, so to intimidate his opponents one of his attendants tied the severed heads to a long stalk of green bamboo and carried it into Katō's fresh conflicts like a general's standard. Katō Kiyomasa was named that day as one of the 'Seven Spears of Shizugatake' – the most valiant warriors, and from that time on his fortunes prospered.

In 1585 Katō Kiyomasa received from Hideyoshi the important role of inspector of taxes, and in 1588 he began a long association with the island of Kyūshū. He was based in the castle town of Kumamoto, where statues of Kiyomasa show him in full armour with a striking helmet design. It was supposed to represent a courtier's cap, and was made by building up a crown of wood and papier mâché on top of a simple helmet bowl. Some portraits of Kiyomasa also show him with an extensive beard, which was quite unusual for a samurai. In contrast to Konishi Yukinaga's Catholicism, Kiyomasa was an adherent of the Nichiren sect of Buddhism, and flew as his battle standard a long white pennant which bore, in characters said to have been written by Nichiren himself, the slogan *Namu Myōho Renge Kyō* (Hail to the Lotus of the Divine Law), the motto and battle cry of his followers. Partly because of their religious differences, but chiefly because of old-fashioned samurai rivalry, there was great enmity between the two leading commanders, and for almost the whole of the campaign the pair fought in different places.

Wakizaka Yasuharu

Wakizaka Yasuharu (1554–1620) was one of Hideyoshi's leading naval commanders during the campaign. Born in 1554, Yasuharu had served Hideyoshi loyally at the battle of Shizugatake in 1583, where he had become another of the 'Seven Spears'. In 1585 he had received in fief the island of Awaji in the Inland Sea, and the notorious whirlpools that are created there under certain tidal conditions must have acquainted him very rapidly with the dangers of seafaring. When the Korean campaign began Wakizaka was one of three commanders placed in charge of naval matters for the Tsushima theatre, and was transferred to land-based duties at Yong'in as soon as the army had landed. He returned to naval command shortly afterwards, and was the loser in the great battle of Hansando. He survived the Korean campaign, fought at Sekigahara in 1600 and immediately afterwards took the castle of Sawayama, the headquarters of the victorious Tokugawa's defeated enemy. For this he was richly rewarded.

KOREA

Chŏng Pal

Chŏng Pal (1553–92) was the first Korean commander to feel the brunt of the Japanese invasion. He passed the state examination for a military career in 1579 and served as a royal messenger and then district magistrate of Kŏje Island before becoming garrison commander of Pusan. Being taken by surprise by the Japanese invasion he organized the defence of Pusan but perished in the fighting.

Yi Sunsin

Admiral Yi Sunsin (1545-98) is Korea's greatest hero, and is one of the outstanding naval commanders in the entire history of the world. He was born in 1545, and received the thorough Confucian education that was so necessary for men of his social station. Yi passed the military service examinations in 1576, after which he was appointed to his first command in Hamgyŏng Province. After a brief spell in a naval command in Chŏlla Province in 1580, he was moved back to the army and saw action against the Jurchens in Hamgyŏng Province in 1583, distinguishing himself in one particular battle beside the Tumen River where he enticed the Jurchens forwards with a false retreat. In 1587 he fell foul of the political and factional rivalry that plagued Korean society, and found himself back in the ranks as a common soldier after annoying General Yi Il. Fortunately for Korea, Yu Sŏngnyong, the future prime minister of Korea, was a rising star at court and had been Yi's boyhood friend, so through Yu's influence Yi was reinstated and new responsibilities soon followed. In 1591, following Yu's recommendation, Yi Sunsin was appointed to the post of Left Naval

Admiral Yi Sunsin is Korea's greatest hero. By a series of naval victories he cut off the Japanese lines of communication and ensured that the retreat set in motion by the Chinese victories ended with a Japanese withdrawal. Statues of Yi Sunsin abound. This one is in the grounds of a school in Ungch'ŏn.

Li Rusong, the distinguished commander of the Chinese armies that liberated Korea, is depicted here in his only defeat. Having recaptured Pyŏngyang, Li was caught in a rearguard action at Pyŏkjeyek to the north of Seoul. He was knocked off his horse and only saved from death by the quick thinking of a subordinate general Li Yousheng. From *Ehon Taikōki*, an illustrated life of Hideyoshi.

Commander of Chŏlla Province, where he threw himself enthusiastically into his duties as the Japanese threat loomed ever nearer. Had Yi been in command in the Pusan area the Japanese landings may never have happened. His naval victories were to prove decisive in the Japanese defeat, although Yi was to die during his final battle in 1598.

Kwŏn Yul

Kwŏn Yul was the outstanding Korean general of the invasion, and stands head and shoulders above his largely incompetent contemporaries. He was promoted from being Magistrate of Kwangju to being commander of Chŏlla Province when the invasion began, and showed a willingness to coordinate his own efforts with those of the irregular forces and the warrior monks. He defeated a Japanese army at the battle of Ich'i, and provided a heroic defence of the mountain fortress of Haengju, a victory that was instrumental in forcing the Japanese to evacuate Seoul.

CHINA

Li Rusong

Dismissed in traditional Japanese accounts of the war for being the loser at the battle of Pyŏkjeyek in 1593, a Japanese victory that did nothing to halt the Japanese evacuation of the capital, Li Rusong was in fact one of Ming China's most accomplished generals. While the Japanese were invading Korea Li Rusong was in command against the rebels in Ningxia, and it is testimony to the high regard in which he was held that the Wanli Emperor had bestowed upon him the title of *tidu* (military superintendent), a position that allowed him direct access to the throne, supreme military command in the field and the power to impeach other officials. His conduct in Ningxia justified the confidence that the Ming emperor had in him, and he was reappointed to the post on taking command of the Korean effort. His recapture of P'yŏngyang was to be the turning point in the Korean campaign, and, although massively defeated in the Japanese rearguard action at Pyŏkjeyek, Li rallied and followed through to drive the Japanese to the coast.

OPPOSING FORCES

JAPAN

The elite troops of the Japanese army were the famous samurai, the knights of old Japan. Traditionally, they had been the only warriors to own and ride horses. Centuries before their primary role had been to act as mounted archers, although this skill was rarely displayed on a battlefield by 1592. Instead their usual weapon was now the *yari* (spear), a weapon unsuitable for slashing but ideal for stabbing – the best technique to use from a saddle. A useful variation was a cross-bladed spear that enabled a samurai to pull an opponent from his horse. If a samurai wished to deliver slashing strokes from horseback then a better choice was the *naginata*, a polearm with a long curved blade, or the spectacular *nodachi*, an extra long sword with a very strong and very long handle. *Yari* would also be the samurai's primary weapon of choice when he had to fight dismounted.

The samurai's other main weapon was of course the famous *katana* – the classic samurai sword. Forged to perfection, and with a razor-sharp edge within a resilient body, this two-handed sword was the finest edged weapon in the history of warfare. Every samurai possessed at least one pair of swords, the standard fighting sword and the shorter *wakizashi*. Contrary to popular belief, both seem to have been carried into battle along with a *tantō* (dagger). The samurai never used shields. Instead the *katana* was both sword and shield, its resilience enabling the samurai to deflect a blow aimed at him by knocking the attacking sword to one side with the flat of the blade and then following up with a stroke of his own.

In the press of battle the swinging of a sword was greatly restricted, and Japanese armour gave good protection, so it was rare for a man to be killed with one sweep of a sword blade. Sword fighting from a horse was not easy, because the normally two-handed sword had to be used in one hand, but this disadvantage was somewhat overcome by the samurai's position above a foot soldier and the momentum of his horse. The process was helped by the curvature of the sword's blade, which allowed the very hard and very sharp cutting edge to slice into an opponent along a small area that would open up to cut through to the bone as the momentum of the swing continued.

By 1592 the traditional style of Japanese armour, whereby armour plates were made from individual lamellae (iron or leather scales) laced together, had become modified to allow solid plate body armours that gave better protection against gunfire. Lamellar sections, however, continued to be found in the thigh guards and shoulder guards. Armoured sleeves for the arm and shinguards protected those areas of the body. An iron mask that provided a secure point for tying the helmet cords protected the face. The mask was often decorated with moustaches made of horsehair, and the mouthpiece might well sport a sinister grin around white teeth! The helmet was a very solid affair, but senior samurai, and many *daimyō* would use the design of the helmet crown to build up the surface of an iron helmet into fantastic shapes.

The other way by which an individual samurai would be recognized in the heat of battle was by wearing on his back a small identifying device called a *sashimono*. This was often a flag in a wooden holder with the *daimyō*'s *mon* (family crest) on a coloured background. This would be the case for most rank-and-file samurai too, but senior samurai would be allowed to have their own *mon*, or sometimes their surname displayed on the flag.

The Japanese army was very well organized. Under Hideyoshi the *ashigaru* (footsoldiers) had finally been integrated into the standing armies of *daimyō* as the lowest ranks of the samurai. They were organized in weapons squads armed with either long spears, harquebuses or bows, while some provided attendance on the *daimyō* or on senior samurai, as grooms, weapon bearers, bodyguards, standard bearers and the like. The *ashigaru* wore simple suits of iron armour that bore the *mon* of the *daimyō*, a device that also appeared on the simple lampshade-shaped helmet and on the flags of the unit. The *ashigaru* were trained to fight in formation. The spearmen provided a defence for the missile troops, and could also act in an offensive capacity with their long spears. The most important Japanese infantry weapon was the harquebus. Its inaccuracy and slowness in reloading was compensated for by the use of massed volley firing, for which the *ashigaru* were highly trained.

CHINA

The timing of the invasion of Korea meant that the Chinese army was required to be in three places at once: the Korean border, the south-west of China where an aboriginal chieftain was carrying out a rebellion, and in Ningxia where the mutiny of Pubei, the last serious Mongol threat to Ming supremacy, had to be suppressed. It is not therefore surprising that the contribution made by the Ming towards the relief of Korea, aid that had been requested even before the Japanese had set sail, should appear to be a case of 'too little, too late'.

The Ming army was certainly not the force it once had been. The traditional system of frontier defence of the early Ming had come to an end after the Tumu Incident of 1449, and the regular army, the core of which consisted of mercenary troops, had deteriorated in both quality and quantity. However, military organization was generally good and well provided with reinforcements which could be moved readily by land. In the Ningxia campaign the Ming army successfully transported 400 artillery pieces over 480km of difficult terrain.

The army had also been reorganized successfully by Qi Jiguang, who had triumphed against the *wakō* and had published a book on military matters in 1567, which later came to the attention of the Koreans. Qi's system, controlled by strict discipline, divided the infantry into five groups: firearms, swordsmen, archers with fire arrows, ordinary archers and spearmen, all of whom were backed up by cavalry and artillery crews. Many of the cavalry were mounted archers, while the Chinese footsoldiers used crossbows and were well supplied with firearms, including harquebuses.

The iron helmet of a Korean officer, ornamented with gold and with a protective neck cover of studded leather and fabric. (Royal Armouries Museum, Leeds)

The basic design of a suit of Chinese armour was made from lamellae of iron or leather made into different sections with a rounded conical iron helmet. Simpler armour consisted of a three-quarter-length heavy coat, reinforced in different ways, and worn over an inner garment that resembled a divided apron, with trousers and leather boots. The coat usually had sleeves, either full sleeves or short ones. The heads of rivets, which held in place small plates inside the armour, protruded from its outside surface to give an appearance very similar to brigandine. Alternatively, a brigandine coat could be made by sewing metal or leather plates so that each overlapped the one below it. Separate shoulder protectors were occasionally used.

Chinese field artillery and siege cannon were the finest in the region. The first Chinese guns were of cast bronze, but cast iron was being used in China from 1356 onwards. A Ming edict of 1412 ordered the stationing of batteries of five cannon at each of the frontier passes as a form of garrison artillery. Some designs of Chinese cannon saw very long service. For example the 'crouching tiger cannon', which dated from 1368, was still being used against the Japanese in Korea in 1592. It was fitted with a curious loose metal collar with two legs so that it needed no external carriage for laying. Another was the 'great general cannon', of which several sizes existed, and an account of 1606 notes that 300 different great general guns were made in 1465. Ye Mengxiong, who lived in the second half of the 16th century, 'changed the weight of the gun to 250 catties [150kg] and doubled its length to six feet, but eliminated the stand and it is now placed on a carriage with wheels. When fired it has a range of 800 paces.' The enthusiastic description continues:

A single shot has the power of thunderbolt, causing several hundred casualties among men and horses. If thousands, or tens of thousands, were placed in position along the frontiers, and every one of them manned by soldiers well trained to use them, then [we should be] invincible. ... At first its heavy weight caused some doubt as to whether or not it was too cumbersome; but if it is transported on its carriage then it is suitable, irrespective of height, distance, or difficulty of terrain.

It is more than likely that great general guns made up much of the 700-piece artillery train that the Ming used in their campaign against rebels in Ningxia in 1592, just prior to joining in the Korean campaign against Japan.

From the early 16th century onwards a different type of gun entered the Chinese arsenal. It was known as the *folang zhi*, which means 'Frankish gun', 'the Franks' being a general term for any inhabitants of the lands to the west, and was of a fundamentally different design from the 'great general', because these new weapons were breech loaders. The ball was placed inside from the breech end, while powder and wad were introduced into the breech inside a sturdy container shaped like a large tankard with a handle. The main disadvantage was leakage around the muzzle and a consequent loss of explosive energy, but this was compensated for by a comparatively high rate of fire, as several breech containers could be prepared in advance.

KOREA

In contrast to Japan, the senior officers of the Korean army tended to be social aristocrats rather than military ones. Several good generals were produced by the system, but there were many bad ones too. The Korean army therefore tended to be loosely organized and quite haphazard. The practice of sending generals from Seoul to command local troops was also a major weakness, while the garrison soldiers were almost totally untrained, disorganized and ill disciplined.

Korea's close proximity to China ensured that the evolution of Korean armour followed that of China rather than Japan. The Korean helmet consisted of a simple rounded conical bowl made from four main pieces riveted together and secured round the brow. A neckguard of lamellae or brigandine was suspended from it in three sections, and decoration in the form of feathers could be flown from the helmet point. Korean foot soldiers wore no armour at all, just their traditional white clothes with a sleeveless black jacket and a belt. A stiffened felt hat gave some small protection in battle.

Early Korean swords were two-edged, straight-bladed weapons, a design that remained popular, although curved swords like Japanese *katana* were also made, and actual Japanese models were imported. By contrast, Korean polearms show considerable Chinese influence. Their use was most prized from the back of a horse, so we see cavalrymen armed with tridents, long straight spears and glaives with heavy curved blades much wider than a Japanese *naginata*. Unique to Korea, however, was the flail, a rounded hardwood stick, painted red and 1.5m long, to which was attached a shorter and heavier mace-like shaft studded with iron nails or knobs. A short length of chain provided the attachment. Foot soldiers were armed with all the above varieties of polearm except the flail. Prowess at archery was greatly valued, and the famous Admiral Yi Sunsin was an accomplished archer. The ordinary Korean bow was a composite reflex bow, made from mulberry wood, bamboo, water buffalo horn and cow sinew spliced together. It had a pronounced negative curve, against which the bow had to be pulled in order to string it. A Japanese source from the time of the 1592 invasion claims that Korean bows were the one thing in which the Koreans were superior to the Japanese, because their range was 450m against the Japanese longbow's range of 300m. However, by this time the Japanese bow had largely been abandoned in favour of the harquebus. Arrows were made of bamboo, but not lacquered after the Japanese fashion. Simple leather quivers were used.

At the time of the Japanese invasions the most marked deficiency in weaponry between Korea and Japan lay in the field of personal firearms. Korea had adopted the Chinese-style handgun a century and a half before it was introduced to Japan, and had developed it into the Korean *sŭngja* (victory gun), a form of simple musket that took the clumsy weapon to its modest peak of perfection. However, the quality and number of Korean cannon provided a direct contrast to the situation that existed with firearms. The heavy cannon used on board Korean ships from the early 15th century onwards had no equivalent in Japan. They could shoot cannon balls of iron or polished stone, but the favourite missile was the wooden arrow, winged with leather and tipped with iron, which caused immense destruction when it

Korean cavalry exercising with halberds, from an illustrated scroll in the War Memorial Museum, Seoul (reproduced by kind permission).

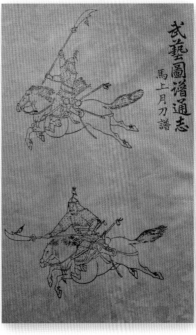

struck the planking of a Japanese vessel. Fire arrows loosed from ordinary bows were also important, and some of the larger cannon-based arrows could be converted into fire arrows. Korea also developed certain specialized weapons of its own. One of the most interesting and effective of these was the mortar, used for firing stones, balls or bombs. The bombs used a clever double-fuse system, a fast burning fuse for the mortar, and a slower one for the bomb itself. The operator would light both fuses simultaneously. For mobility the mortars, which came in three basic sizes, were mounted on wooden carriages. The other innovative Korean weapon was the curious armoured artillery vehicle called a *hwach'a* (fire wagon), which fired a volley of rockets.

Korea's greatest strength lay with its navy. The standard fighting ship the *p'anoksŏn* may not have been much better than the equivalent Japanese vessel, but had a vast superiority in firepower from cannon. The famous turtle ships became the pride of the fleet, although their numbers seem to have been small during the Japanese campaign. There is no space here to describe the turtle ships in detail, as I did in New Vanguard 63: *Fighting Ships of the Far East Volume 2* (Osprey Publishing Ltd: Oxford, 2003), but it is important to note that the actual design of the turtle ship is still controversial. Until recently it was assumed that it was much longer than it was wide. This is how it is commonly represented, but it is now believed that it may have been almost literally turtle shaped to account for its manoeuvrability. Arguments have also been put forward to claim that it must have been three-decked, not two-decked, so that the artillerymen on the upper deck did not interfere with the oarsmen on the lower deck.

ORDERS OF BATTLE

Detailed orders of battle are only available for the Japanese side. Chinese and Korean numbers will be given as appropriate in the description of individual actions.

The numbers of Japanese troops who took part in the invasion are well documented, although there are small discrepancies between different sets of figures, which are largely explained by the inclusion or omission of reserve corps from the various lists. The most reliable source, an order of battle sent by Hideyoshi to Mōri Terumoto, gives an overall structure of vanguard, main body, rearguard and reserves, totalling approximately 158,800 men. Hideyoshi's plans envisioned that the First Division would establish a bridgehead at Pusan under Konishi Yukinaga, who was to be joined by the Second Division under Katō Kiyomasa for the drive north. The final vanguard unit, the Third Division under Kuroda Nagamasa, was to attack to the west of Pusan across the Naktong River. They were to be joined within a few days by the Fourth, Fifth, Sixth and Seventh divisions totalling 84,700 men, while the Eighth and Ninth Divisions of 21,500 men were to be held in immediate reserve on the islands of Tsushima and Iki respectively. When war began the Ninth Division was moved forwards to Tsushima. There was also a sizeable rearguard left in reserve in Japan, named in some accounts as the Tenth Division, while Hizen-Nagoya Castle was garrisoned by 27,000 troops under Hideyoshi's personal command, together with over 70,000 men supplied by the eastern *daimyō* who stayed in reserve in the castle town. Even those who did not expect to see their forces cross the seas suffered some disruption with the stationing of thousands more as the final rearguard near Kyoto. A whole nation was at war.

BLITZKRIEG ON KOREA

Konishi Yukinaga sets sail for Korea. The Japanese ships, which had little in the way of defensive armaments, are shown here ploughing through the seas on their way to make the first landfall in Korea. From *Ehon Taikōki*, an illustrated life of Hideyoshi.

The first shots of the Korean campaign were fired against the defences of Pusan, the vast natural harbour that is still South Korea's main port. Having travelled via Iki and Tsushima, the Japanese fleet rested overnight in Pusan Harbour, completely unmolested by the Korean navy, whose local commander, Wǒn Kyun, was an incompetent coward. Dividing their forces, Konishi Yukinaga and Sō Yoshitomo led simultaneous early morning attacks against the main city walls of Pusan and a subsidiary harbour fort called Tadaejin, a strategy planned because of the local knowledge possessed by Sō Yoshitomo.

Sō Yoshitomo's attack on Pusan was countered by Chǒng Pal, the Pusan commander, who had been hunting on Yǒng Island off Pusan Harbour when the invasion fleet was spotted. He rushed back to his post, and a Korean account, which refers to the Japanese only as 'the robbers', relates how Pusan held out as long as it could, its garrison killing many Japanese before being overwhelmed. 'In one day', it notes, 'the bodies of the robbers had piled up like a mountain. However, at length the arrows were exhausted and all they could do was wait for reinforcements.' At that moment Chǒng Pal was suddenly hit by a bullet and died. Chǒng Pal thus became the first senior Korean casualty of the invasion, and is commemorated today in Pusan by a statue that stands, appropriately enough, next to the Japanese Consulate.

Dressed in his distinctive black armour, the brave Chŏng Pal, the commander of Pusan, is killed during the attack by Sō Yoshitomo. He was the first senior Korean casualty of the invasion. (From a painting in the Ch'ungyŏlsa Shrine, Tongnae, by kind permission)

Morale collapsed with his death, and Pusan soon fell. Chŏng Pal's concubine wept when she heard of his death and committed suicide next to his dead body. Even Chŏng Pal's servant attacked the Japanese lines and was killed. Afterwards one Japanese general commented, 'Among the generals of your country, the general of Pusan dressed in black must have been the most feared general of all.'

With the death of the 'brave general dressed in black' the Japanese army completed its first objective. Meanwhile, Konishi Yukinaga was leading the assault on the harbour fort of Tadaejin. Rocks and lumber were flung into the moats and ditches, and bamboo scaling ladders were raised for an assault under the cover of volleys of gunfire. Yun Hŭngsin defended Tadaejin bravely, but the castle soon fell and every member of the garrison was put to the sword.

A rapid advance towards Seoul began. A few kilometres to the north of Pusan lay the fortress of Tongnae. Unlike Pusan, Tongnae was a *sansŏng* (mountain castle) that dominated the main road north towards Seoul. After resting overnight at Pusan, the First Division left at 6am the following morning and began the attack on Tongnae two hours later. The battle provided Korea with its third heroic martyr of the war. Its governor was called Song Sanghyŏn, and it was to this brave young man that Konishi Yukinaga presented anew the Japanese demands for a clear road through to China. It was again rejected with the words, 'It is easy for me to die, but difficult to let you pass', so for a third time the ramparts of a Korean castle were swept with bullets. A few weeks a later a liberated Korean prisoner of war described the battle to Admiral Yi Sunsin in these words:

The Japanese gathered in countless numbers and surrounded the city wall in five lines with other troops crowding into the nearby fields. The vanguard, consisting of about 100 men, wearing helmets and armour and each holding a tall ladder, dashed to the city wall together with others and placed bamboo ladders and climbed over the ramparts in many places.

The man added that after the fall of Tongnae many people were killed, which implies a massacre similar to that which had happened at Pusan, where an orgy of indiscriminate killing had even included the beheading of dogs and cats.

Sō Yoshitomo then sent out a small group of samurai with ten *ashigaru* to scout the position of Yangsan Castle, the next strongpoint on the road towards Seoul that covered the Naktong River. On drawing near, the ten *ashigaru* fired a volley from their harquebuses, which so terrified the defenders of Yangsan that they immediately abandoned the castle and fled. Yangsan was occupied at dawn the following morning, so the front line of the Japanese bridgehead was moved farther north with ease.

The first invasion, 1592, and the retreat to Seoul, 1593

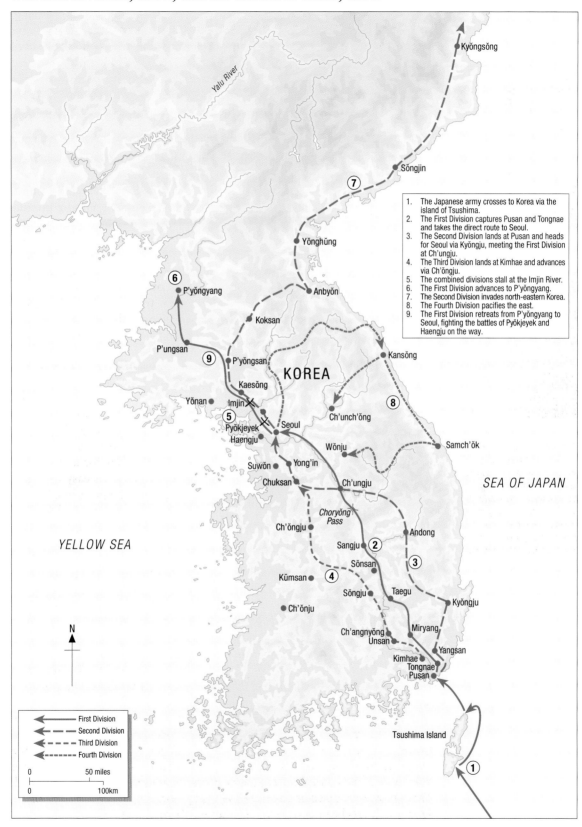

1. The Japanese army crosses to Korea via the island of Tsushima.
2. The First Division captures Pusan and Tongnae and takes the direct route to Seoul.
3. The Second Division lands at Pusan and heads for Seoul via Kyŏngju, meeting the First Division at Ch'ungju.
4. The Third Division lands at Kimhae and advances via Ch'ŏngju.
5. The combined divisions stall at the Imjin River.
6. The First Division advances to P'yŏngyang.
7. The Second Division invades north-eastern Korea.
8. The Fourth Division pacifies the east.
9. The First Division retreats from P'yŏngyang to Seoul, fighting the battles of Pyŏkjeyek and Haengju on the way.

That afternoon, Konishi Yukinaga's main body left Tongnae, passed Yangsan and headed for the next castle on the road, which was Miryang. There was a minor skirmish en route and Miryang was occupied. The next strongpoint, Taegu, had been deliberately denuded of troops because of the Korean decision to make a stand farther north. Konishi Yukinaga led his army in a crossing of the undefended Naktong River, where his scouts brought him news that a Korean army was waiting for him at the fortress of Sangju. By now the First Division had been on Korean soil for 11 days. They had met virtually no opposition since leaving Tongnae, and had advanced beyond what would have been reasonable limits of safety had it not been for the fact that both the Second and Third divisions had now landed and were covering their flanks to the right and left. A disastrous Korean defeat followed at Ch'ungju. On arriving outside Seoul the capital city was found to have been abandoned. The Korean king had fled to P'yŏngyang, shocked by the sudden collapse of his country's resistance.

The rapidity of the initial Japanese successes meant that certain officials in the Ming court began to suspect that Korea had abandoned its tributary relationship with China and were actually aiding the Japanese. The Wanli Emperor was so concerned about this that he dispatched an envoy to P'yŏngyang who returned with the news that the loyal Koreans had simply been overcome by sheer force of arms and urgently required Chinese assistance. Wanli was keen to comply, but the Ningxia Mutiny was still raging so all the Chinese could do was to urge the Koreans to hang on as best they could until a Ming army was ready. This was easier said than done, but the Japanese invaders gave the Koreans an unexpected respite shortly after taking Seoul by failing to cross the Imjin River until a Korean raid disclosed its fordable areas.

The assault on the detached harbour fortress of Tadaejin by Konishi Yukinaga. (From a hanging scroll in Pusan Municipal Museum, by kind permission)

The Japanese army also unwittingly helped the Chinese by dividing their army in two. Konishi Yukinaga pressed on towards the north along the shortest route to the Chinese border via P'yŏngyang, while his rival Katō Kiyomasa set off on a long campaign to pacify the north-east of Korea. This had some strategic merit because it would cover the eastern flank of any advance into China. At that time Nurhaci (1559–1616), the leader of the Manchurian Jurchens who would eventually overthrow the Ming dynasty in favour of the Later Jin/Qing dynasty (1644–1911), was the Ming's ally. Katō Kiyomasa succeeded in this objective. A system of taxation and land surveys on the Japanese model followed, interspersed by attacks on Korean fortresses and a brief incursion into Manchuria, but Kiyomasa's adventure really helped only to diminish the continuing impact of the Japanese invasion, which stalled after Konishi Yukinaga had captured P'yŏngyang. The Korean king fled to the Yalu River and was ready to escape into China whenever the last Japanese push against Korea began. But no further move north was made, and P'yŏngyang was destined to be the last outpost of this new Japanese empire.

A fierce counterattack is launched from Pusan against Sō Yoshitomo. (From a painting in the Ch'ungyŏlsa Shrine, Tongnae, by kind permission)

27

THE JAPANESE CAPTURE THE FORTRESS OF PUSAN FROM THE KOREANS UNDER CHŎNG PAL: 1592 (pp. 28–29)

The harbour fortress of Pusan was part of the city wall, and was the first place to be attacked following the Japanese landing. In this plate we are looking from just inside the main gate as the first Japanese assault breaks in. The fortified gateway is built in typical Korean style, derived from contemporary China, whereby the actual entrance is a dark tunnel with a heavy gate through a stone and brick wall (1). On top of the gateway is an ornate gatehouse pavilion (2). Instead of fighting their way in through the gate the Japanese have however surmounted the wall using scaling ladders under the cover provided by hundreds of harquebus troops firing volleys of bullets. The Japanese assault parties are in small groups. In the background a Korean unit lead a counterattack up the stone steps to the gatehouse.

The troops are led by Sō Yoshitomo, *daimyō* of Tsushima. Yoshitomo whose family had ancient connections with Korea played a prominent role in the negotiations and planning prior to the invasion and is suitably dressed for the leader of the first attack. Over his bullet-proof armour he wears a *jinbaori* (surcoat), and from his back there flies a flag bearing his *mon* (badge), which is identical to that used by his commander-in-chief Toyotomi Hideyoshi (3). Similar flags are worn by his

samurai on the backs of their armour. The *ashigaru* (footsoldiers) have the badge on their simple helmets. They also wear plain suits of armour over short-sleeved shirts to help them in the summer heat. The Japanese protective costume is however very sophisticated when compared with the almost total lack of protection provided for the Korean foot soldiers. Their stiffened felt hats are the only defence they have against the Japanese swords. Otherwise they are dressed in plain cloth jackets and trousers.

The only proper Korean armour is seen on the Korean officers, who wear heavy coats inside of which are leather plates, reinforced here and there with metal studs. Like their iron helmets these armours are very Chinese in appearance. The fierce resistance is under the leadership of Chŏng Pal (4), commander of Pusan, who is dressed in his distinctive black armour and is fighting under his personal standard carried by a foot soldier (5). Even this attendant to the general is very lightly armed. The plate is based on an oil painting hanging in the museum of the Ch'ungyŏlsa Shrine in Tongnae, where the defenders of Pusan are commemorated.

THE WAR AT SEA

When Korea began to hit back at the Japanese the first successes were achieved at sea. Korea's first victory of the invasion was the battle of Okp'o, a naval battle fought by Admiral Yi Sunsin off the east coast of Kŏje Island. As with so many of Yi's operations, we have a full and detailed account in his own words written as a memorial to court. 'Yi, Your Majesty's humble subject, Commander of Chŏlla Left Naval Station,' he begins, 'memorializes the throne on the slaughter of the enemy.' Having sent a message to Right Commander Yi Ŏk-ki to follow him, Yi set sail under cover of darkness at 2.00am at the head of 24 *p'anoksŏn*, 15 smaller fighting vessels, and 46 other boats. The fleet travelled for the whole of that day, entering the waters of Kyŏngsang Province at sunset, where he anchored for the night.

At dawn two days later, the fleet rounded the south coast of Kŏje Island and headed towards Kadŏk Island, where Japanese ships had been seen gathering, but while they were on their way Yi's scouting vessels announced the discovery of 50 Japanese ships lying off the harbour of Okp'o on the eastern coast of Kŏje. As with most of these encounters, it is by no means clear who the Japanese units actually were, but their purpose was clear. Having no opposing armies to fight they were carrying out their mission to pacify Kyŏngsang by looting and burning the nearby port like their *wakō* ancestors. At that point the Japanese saw the Korean warships through the smoke that rose above the mountain crests, and ran about in great confusion, trying to regain their boats and man their oars. The fleet lifted anchor, but hugged the shore rather than heading for the open sea. Yi's ships encircled the fleeing Japanese and bombarded them with cannon balls, wooden arrows and fire arrows. The Japanese returned their fire with harquebuses and bows, but the Korean tactic of attacking from a distance did not allow them any opportunity to board. They threw their stores overboard and jumped into the water to swim to the shore, while the survivors scattered over the rocky cliffs. A girl captive of the Japanese became an eyewitness to the battle of Okp'o:

> Cannon balls and long arrows poured down like hail on the Japanese vessels from our ships. Those who were struck by the missiles fell dead, bathed in blood, while others rolled on deck with wild shrieks or jumped into the water to climb up to the hills. At that time I remained motionless with fear in the bottom of the boat for long hours, so I did not know what was happening in the outside world.

Resisting the temptation to send parties ashore to mop up survivors, Yi pulled his fleet back to the open sea, and preparations were being made to spend the night when five more Japanese ships were spotted. The Korean fleet gave chase and caught up with them near the mainland at Ungch'ŏn. Deserting their ships the Japanese hurried ashore, at which the Korean ships moved in and destroyed four out of the five with cannon and fire arrows. When it grew dark Yi pulled away and spent the night at sea. Twenty-six Japanese vessels had been sunk on that first day. The following morning reports were received that more Japanese ships had been sighted to the west. The Koreans destroyed 11 out of these 13 ships. Certain articles taken from the Japanese ships greatly amused Yi, who was particularly intrigued by the Japanese habit of wearing elaborately ornamented helmets:

> The red-black Japanese armour, iron helmets, horse manes, gold crowns, gold fleece, gold armour, feather dress, feather brooms, shell trumpets and many other curious things in strange shapes with rich ornaments strike onlookers with awe, like weird ghosts or strange beasts.

Not wishing to exclude King Sŏnjo from such wonders, Yi forwarded with his report 'one armoured gun barrel and one left ear cut from a Japanese beheaded by Sin Ho, Magistrate of Nagan'.

The battle of Okp'o was fought without the loss of a single Korean ship, and caused consternation among the Japanese command when the news spread to newly conquered Seoul. At the time the stand-off at the Imjin River was still continuing, and a defeat in their rear was not what the Japanese generals wanted to hear.

Japanese invaders, shown to look very much like the *wakō* of old, gather outside the gate of Tongnae. (From a hanging scroll in Pusan Municipal Museum, by kind permission)

THE BATTLE OF SACH'ŎN AND THE TURTLE SHIP

The people Yi interviewed after the Okp'o actions provided ample proof of the savagery of Japan's pacification process along the coast of Kyŏngsang and, following his initial victory, Yi was naturally determined to take the fight to the enemy again. His original intention was to mount a major sea offensive, but on receiving a report that Japanese vessels had been sighted as far west as Sach'ŏn, which lay very near the border with Chŏlla Province, Yi realized that he had to act swiftly, because it was very likely that ground troops were advancing along the coast as well.

It appeared that many Japanese ships were moored in the bay of Sach'ŏn below a promontory on which a Japanese commander had merely set up his command post. Yi knew his arrows would not reach the Japanese on the hill, and that the ebbing tide made it most unwise for the *p'anoksŏn* to sail in for close-range artillery fire. It was also getting dark, but the one encouraging sign was the extreme arrogance being shown by the Japanese. If they could be persuaded to display further annoyance by

Han Kŭkham was defeated by Katō Kiyomasa at a large grain storehouse by the sea near Sŏngjin (modern Kimch'aek). His army was pursued afterwards, and this illustration shows Han himself being chased by a samurai intent on taking his head. The samurai wears a *horō* (cloak) and is swinging a grappling hook on a rope. From *Ehon Taikōki*, an illustrated life of Hideyoshi.

chasing the Korean fleet out on to the open sea then the situation could be very different. The Korean navy therefore turned tail and appeared to flee. As if on cue hundreds of Japanese poured down from the Sach'ŏn heights and leapt into their ships for a hot pursuit. By the time they caught up with the Koreans the tide had turned, and it is at this crucial point that we first read of the use in battle of Yi Sunsin's secret weapon. 'Previously, foreseeing the Japanese invasion,' he writes modestly in his report to King Sŏnjo about the battle of Sach'ŏn, 'I had a turtle ship made. …' It was fitted:

> … with a dragon's head, from whose mouth we could fire our cannons, and with iron spikes on its back to pierce the enemy's feet when they tried to board. Because it is in the shape of a turtle, our men can look out from inside, but the enemy cannot look in from outside. It moves so swiftly that it can plunge into the midst of even many hundreds of enemy vessels in any weather to attack them with cannon balls and fire throwers.

A particularly brave captain was chosen to command the turtle ship on its first outing, and he led it as the Korean navy's vanguard when they counter-attacked, firing a selection of cannon balls, wooden arrows and fire arrows into the Japanese fleet. All the Japanese ships that had followed them out of the bay were sunk or burned in spite of fierce resistance, but when the fighting was at its height a lone Japanese sharpshooter nearly changed the course of Asian history by putting a bullet through Yi's left shoulder. The wound was not serious, and with the coming of night the Korean fleet calmly withdrew.

THE BATTLES OF TANGP'O AND TANGHANGP'O

The turtle ship saw action for a second time at the battle of Tangp'o off the south-western coast of Mirŭk Island. Once again it was the same pattern of a Japanese squadron lying at anchor to cover the looting and burning of a town. There were 21 Japanese ships in all, and their formation was dominated by a large flagship where sat a senior Japanese commander. He is usually identified

The naval campaign of 1592, showing the battles of Okp'o, Sach'ŏn, Tangp'o, Tanghangp'o, Hansando and Angolp'o, and the raids of Ungch'ŏn and Pusan

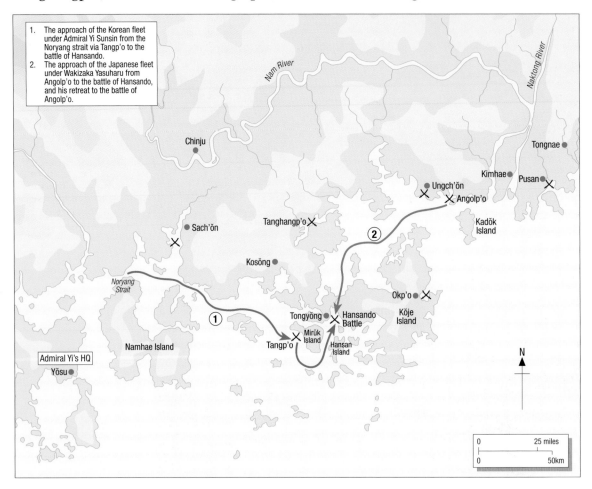

1. The approach of the Korean fleet under Admiral Yi Sunsin from the Noryang strait via Tangp'o to the battle of Hansando.
2. The approach of the Japanese fleet under Wakizaka Yasuharu from Angolp'o to the battle of Hansando, and his retreat to the battle of Angolp'o.

as Kurushima Michiyuki, from a branch of the great pirate family of Murakami. Whatever his identity, the interviews which Yi conducted after the victory with released Korean prisoners leave no doubt about how the man died, and include a remarkable eyewitness account by a Korean girl who had been captured by the Japanese and forced to be the commander's mistress. 'On the day of the battle', she related, 'arrows and bullets rained on the pavilion vessel where he sat. First he was hit on the brow but was unshaken, but when an arrow pierced his chest he fell down with a loud cry.'

The hail of arrows and bullets came chiefly from the turtle ship, which 'dashed close to this pavilion vessel and broke it by shooting cannon balls from the dragon mouth, and by pouring down arrows and cannon balls from other cannon'. It was an archer on a *p'anoksŏn* who put an arrow into the Japanese commander, at which a Korean naval officer cut off the prestigious victim's head with a stroke of his sword. The loss of Kurushima Michiyuki was a decisive blow to Japanese morale, and nearly all the Japanese ships were subsequently sunk or burned.

For the next two days Yi's fleet searched the islands, beaches and straits of the complex sea lanes of Korea's southern coast for signs of the enemy, whom they found at Tanghangp'o, a wide bay across the peninsula from Kosŏng that

LEFT
Admiral Yi Sunsin's naval victory at the battle of Sach'ŏn was the first battle at which the turtle ship was used. In this painting in the Hansando Museum Yi is shown tending the wound he received on his arm.

BELOW, LEFT
The naval battle fought in Pusan Harbour by Admiral Yi Sunsin convinced the Japanese invaders of the importance of coastal defence against the Korean navy. In this diorama in Pusan Municipal Museum a turtle ship is depicted.

was entered to the north-west by a narrow gulf. Twenty-six Japanese ships lay at anchor. At the sight of the Korean ships the Japanese opened a heavy fire, so Yi's fleet held back in a circle spearheaded by the turtle ship, which penetrated the enemy line and rammed the Japanese flagship. The other Korean ships then joined in with cannon and arrow fire, but Yi realized that if the Japanese were driven back they might escape to land, so he again tried a false retreat to draw them on. Once again the ruse worked:

> Then our ships suddenly enveloped the enemy craft from the four directions, attacking them from both flanks at full speed. The turtle with the Flying Squadron Chief on board rammed the enemy's pavilion vessel once again, while wrecking it with cannon fire, and our other ships hit its brocade curtains and sails with fire arrows. Furious flames burst out and the enemy commander fell dead from an arrow hit.

A pursuit of the escaping ships began and continued until nightfall with the destruction of all the Japanese vessels except one and the taking of 43 heads.

The one ship to escape was apprehended by a Korean warship the following morning and a fierce fight ensued. The Japanese captain 'stood alone holding a long sword in his hand and fought to the last without fear', and it was only when ten arrows had been shot into him that 'he shouted loudly and fell, and his head was cut off'. Yi sent as proof to King Sŏnjo the ears his men had cut off from 88 heads, 'salted and packed in a box for shipment to the court'. This was almost the same day that Konishi Yukinaga had captured P'yŏngyang, but on the seas the position of the two contending forces was totally reversed.

THE BATTLE OF HANSANDO

The battle of Hansando (Hansan Island) was Yi Sunsin's greatest victory, and came about because Hideyoshi had ordered Yi's destruction following the reversals described above. The *Wakizaka ki* (the chronicle of the Wakizaka family) contains the text of the order given by Hideyoshi after the debacle at Tanghangp'o to recall Wakizaka and his fellow admirals Katō Yoshiaki and Kuki Yoshitaka from land duties. Their mission was to assemble a fleet and seek out Yi Sunsin to destroy him.

Katō Yoshiaki (1563–1631), who was no relation to the other Katō, had also been one of the illustrious 'Seven Spears of Shizugatake'. The third member of the trio, Kuki Yoshitaka (1542–1600) was the only one who had real naval experience because he had once been a pirate operating on the Pacific coast. During the early days of the Korean invasion Kuki had shared the Tsushima command with Wakizaka, but now that there was the prospect of real action such willingness to share responsibilities rapidly disappeared. Wakizaka's fleet was ready, but neither Katō nor Kuki had enough time to assemble the number of ships they felt they needed for the operation. Being eager for personal glory, Wakizaka decided to act alone instead of waiting until they were all ready. The *Wakizaka ki* implies that the challenge from Admiral Yi was too pressing to consider any delay in responding, but it is more than likely that Wakizaka merely seized the opportunity to gain the personal honour of being the commander who single-handedly destroyed the Korean fleet. He therefore set sail from Angolp'o without his colleagues but with a fleet of 82 ships, including 36 large and 24 medium-sized vessels.

The ensuing struggle takes its name from the island of Hansan near to which it was fought, so the battle, which was both the Salamis and the Trafalgar of Korea, is usually called the battle of Hansando, although Japanese sources usually refer to it by another local geographical feature and call it the battle of Kyŏnnaeryang. Like Okp'o, the overall action included a follow-up operation, which is called by both sides the battle of Angolp'o. This latter engagement was fought against the joint commands of Katō and Kuki, who had by then sailed to join Wakizaka.

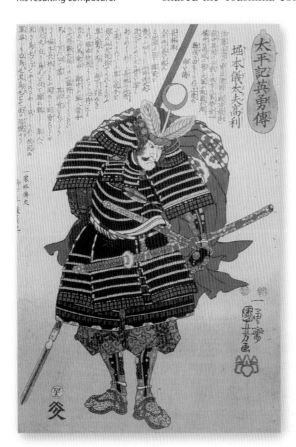

While Morimoto Hidetora was fighting in north-eastern Korea under Katō Kiyomasa's command he received an arrow through his left elbow. Unperturbed, he asked a colleague to withdraw the arrow, and then galloped off anew against the enemy. This print by Kuniyoshi captures his Zen-like detachment from the pain of the wound and his resulting composure.

A turtle ship appears in this painting of the battle of Okp'o in the Ok'po Memorial Museum on Kŏje Island, even though the famous vessel did not make an appearance until the battle of Sach'ŏn.

Yi begins his report to King Sŏnjo with his assessment of the situation prior to the battle. Japanese ships still controlled the sea area between Pusan and the islands of Kadŏk and Kŏje, but had not ventured any farther west since the Tanghangp'o operation. Yet there was a worrying development on land. Yi had heard that Japanese troops had captured Kŭmsan. This meant that they were poised to make their first inroads into Chŏlla Province from the north, and up to that time Yi's homeland of Chŏlla had been the only province still free of invaders. As naval support along the coast of Chŏlla would be vital to the Japanese advance, Yi decided on a large-scale search and destroy operation against the Japanese fleet that he confidently expected to find.

The combined fleets of the Chŏlla stations made rendezvous with Wŏn Kyun in the straits of Noryang off Namhae Island. Unfortunately no Korean records exist of the total numbers of the combined Korean fleets, but Japanese accounts suggest that it was probably around 100 ships. The following day they continued eastwards in the face of a hostile gale, and anchored off Tangp'o, the site of their previous victory, where they took on water. On seeing them a local man came running down to the beach with the news that a large Japanese fleet had been spotted nearby. The Japanese ships had sailed south-west into the narrow straits of Kyŏnnaeryang that divided Kŏje Island from the mainland and had anchored there for the night. Contact was made early the following morning when Yi's fleet headed for the straits and counted 82 enemy vessels.

Nowadays one can stand next to the statue of Admiral Yi Sunsin on top of the hill that overlooks the port of Tongyŏng and look out across this bay where the whole of the battle of Hansando took place. To the south lies the island of Mirŭk, and to the south-east, framing the horizon of the bay, is Hansan Island itself, with several islets dotted about before it. Yi's strategy was determined by the fact that the channel of Kyŏnnaeryang was narrow and strewn with sunken rocks, so it was not only difficult to fight in the bay for fear the Korean ships might collide with one another but provided the likelihood that the Japanese would escape to land. Yi therefore decided to try his well-rehearsed manoeuvre of a false retreat to lure the Japanese out to the south-west, where a wide expanse of sea fringed by several uninhabited islands would provide an ideal location for a sea battle.

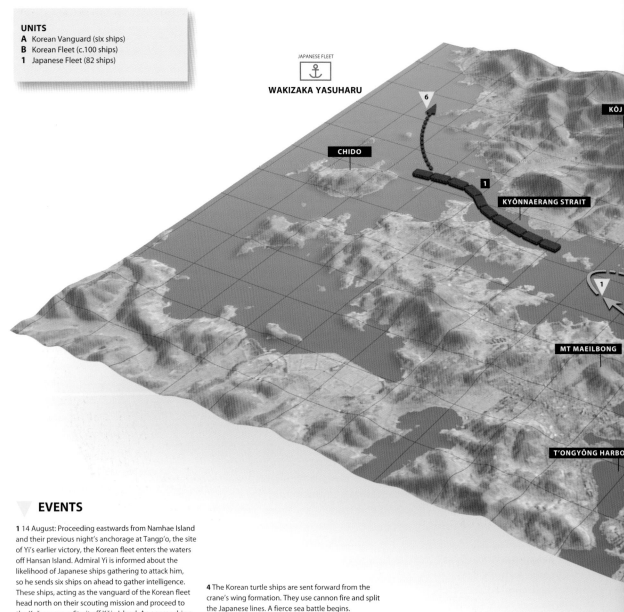

UNITS
A Korean Vanguard (six ships)
B Korean Fleet (c.100 ships)
1 Japanese Fleet (82 ships)

JAPANESE FLEET

WAKIZAKA YASUHARU

CHIDO

KÔJ

KYÔNNAERANG STRAIT

MT MAEILBONG

T'ONGYÔNG HARBO

▼ EVENTS

1 14 August: Proceeding eastwards from Namhae Island and their previous night's anchorage at Tangp'o, the site of Yi's earlier victory, the Korean fleet enters the waters off Hansan Island. Admiral Yi is informed about the likelihood of Japanese ships gathering to attack him, so he sends six ships on ahead to gather intelligence. These ships, acting as the vanguard of the Korean fleet head north on their scouting mission and proceed to the Kyônnaerang Strait off Kôje Island. An approaching Japanese fleet of 82 ships under the command of Wakizaka Yasuharu is observed. They are heading south on a mission to destroy the Korean fleet. The Korean vanguard of six ships executes a false retreat, hoping that the Japanese will follow them. After little hesitation the Japanese fleet, led by Wakizaka Yasuharu follows in hot pursuit.

2 The vanguard of the Korean fleet rejoins the main body near Hansan Island. Admiral Yi takes advantage of his local knowledge and gives orders to receive the Japanese attack. The Korean fleet is deployed in the crane's wing formation ready for the Japanese arrival.

3 The Japanese sail straight ahead into the Korean trap and are surrounded.

4 The Korean turtle ships are sent forward from the crane's wing formation. They use cannon fire and split the Japanese lines. A fierce sea battle begins.

5 The Korean use of cannon begins to give Korea the advantage, although there is also much hand-to-hand fighting when the ships are boarded. Two high-ranking Japanese commanders, Wakizaka Sabei and Wakizaka Shichi'emon are killed on board their ships.

6 Wakizaka Yasuharu orders a full retreat. The 14 surviving vessels of the Japanese fleet head north. Admiral Yi allows them to escape as far as Angolp'o, then follows in pursuit. Another battle takes place on 16 August at Angolp'o.

7 17 August, noon: Admiral Yi returns to Hansando after his second victory to find Japanese survivors on the shores of the tiny islands round about. Many have been without food and water.

THE BATTLE OF HANSANDO (HANSAN ISLAND), 1592
The Korean fleet under Admiral Yi Sunsin inflicts a catastrophic defeat on the Japanese fleet

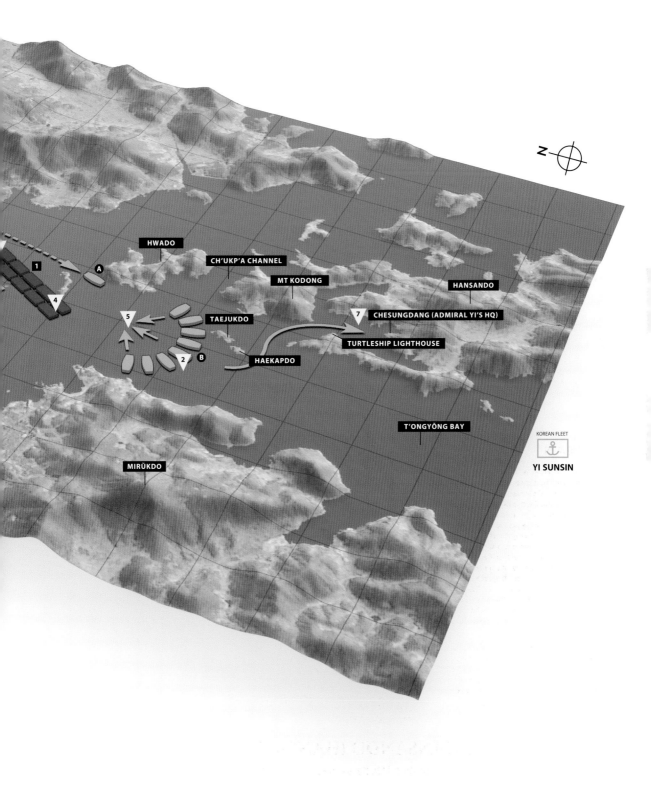

N

HWADO

CH'UKP'A CHANNEL

1

A

MT KODONG

HANSANDO

4

5

TAEJUKDO

7

CHESUNGDANG (ADMIRAL YI'S HQ)

TURTLESHIP LIGHTHOUSE

2

B

HAEKAPDO

T'ONGYŎNG BAY

KOREAN FLEET

MIRŬKDO

YI SUNSIN

The bait was taken, and from the north-east came Yi's vanguard of six *p'anoksŏn*, beating down the straits of Kyŏnnaeryang with Wakizaka Yasuharu's entire fleet in hot pursuit. When the Japanese were well clear of the rocky strait and out into the bay before Hansan Island they found Yi's main body waiting for them. Here the Korean ships had spread out into a semicircular formation which Yi's report calls a 'crane's wing'. The *Wakizaka ki* tells this part of the story as follows: 'The guard ships passed through the middle of the strait and out into a wide area. We took to our oars, at which they spread out their ships like a winnowing fan, drew our ships on and enveloped them.'

By the time of the battle of Hansando the number of turtle ships appears to have grown to at least three, because references to them in Yi's account clearly indicate a plural, and the Japanese account noted below counts three. With the turtles acting as the vanguard once again, the Korean fleet rowed towards the focal point of their crane's-wing formation.

'Then I roared "Charge!"', writes Yi, 'Our ships dashed forward with the roar of cannon breaking two or three of the enemy vessels into pieces'. The fight now became a bloody free-for-all, the Korean ships trying initially to keep their chosen victims at a distance in order to bombard the Japanese without the risk of a boarding party being sent against them. Much hand-to-hand fighting took place, but Yi allowed this only if the Japanese vessel was already crippled. Thus we read that 'Left Flying Squadron Chief [a turtle boat captain] Yi Kinam captured one enemy vessel and cut off seven Japanese heads', and a certain Chŏng Un, captain from Nokdo, 'holed and destroyed two large enemy pavilion vessels with cannon fire and burned them completely by attacks in cooperation with other ships, cut off three Japanese heads, and rescued two Korean prisoners of war.' The greatest glory, however, fell to two individuals:

> Sunch'ŏn magistrate Kwŏn Chun, forgetting all about himself, penetrated the enemy position first, breaking and capturing one large enemy pavilion vessel, and beheading ten Japanese warriors including the Commander, and bringing back a Korean prisoner of war. Kwangyang Magistrate Ŏ Yŏngtam also dashed forward, breaking and capturing one large pavilion vessel. He hit the enemy Commander with an arrow, and brought him back to my ship, but before interrogation, he fell dead without speaking, so I ordered his head to be cut off.

The view looking from beside the monument to Admiral Yi Sunsin above the town of T'ongyŏng towards the island of Hansan. The battle of Hansando was fought within this area of sea.

A detail showing a turtle ship from a diorama depicting the battle of Hansando in the War Memorial Museum, Seoul.

The 'commanders' in the above paragraph probably indicates the captains of the individual ships concerned, but is it known that two people related to the overall commander Wakizaka Yasuharu were killed at Hansando, and the *Wakizaka ki* gives their names as Wakizaka Sabei and Watanabe Shichi'emon. Yasuharu himself had a very narrow escape:

> However, as Yasuharu was on board a fast ship with many oars he attacked and withdrew freely to safety. Arrows struck against his armour but he was unafraid even though there were ten dead for every one living and the enemy ships were attacking all the more fiercely. As it was being repeatedly attacked by fire arrows, Yasuharu's fast ship was finally made to withdraw …

Unlike Wakizaka, one ship's captain could not face the dishonour of withdrawal: 'A man called Manabe Samanosuke was a ship's captain that day, and the ship he was on was set on fire. This tormented him, and saying that he could not face meeting the other samurai in the army again, committed suicide and died.'

The *Wakizaka ki* also adds some detail about the Korean attacks, mentioning that the Japanese fleet was bombarded with metal-cased fire bombs shot from mortars similar to those used in Korean sieges. These weapons would probably have been fired from the open *p'anoksŏn* rather than from the confined space of a turtle ship.

The destruction of Wakizaka's fleet was almost total. Hardly a single ship escaped, and 'countless numbers of Japanese were hit by arrows and fell dead into the water', but not all were killed, because '… about four hundred exhausted Japanese finding no way to escape, deserted their boats and fled ashore'. The victorious Koreans, similarly exhausted, withdrew for the night.

Thus ended the first phase of the most severe defeat to be suffered by a Japanese force in the entire Korean campaign, but the battle of Hansando had a sequel, because the two colleagues whom Wakizaka had left behind had hurried after him to secure their share of the glory. Leaving Pusan on the day of the battle of Hansando, they were apprised of the disaster that same evening. One chronicle tells it rather differently, and reads 'The two men Kuki Yoshitaka and Katō Yoshiaki heard tell of the distinguished service performed

A view from Hansan Island showing the lighthouse built in the shape of a turtle ship. The main action of the battle of Hansando took place beyond the rock on which the lighthouse was built as a memorial.

by Wakizaka Yasuharu', but whatever their motivation, their fleet reached only as far as the port of Angolp'o to which Wakizaka had withdrawn in defeat. Hindered by an unfavourable wind, Yi Sunsin had to wait one full day before pursuing Wakizaka and coming to grips with Kuki and Katō at the battle of Angolp'o.

Yi Sunsin headed for the harbour to make a reconnaissance in force. Sailing forwards in the crane's-wing formation, with Wŏn Kyun's ships following closely behind, Yi found 42 Japanese ships lying at anchor with the protection of nearby land and shallow waters around. An attempt at a false retreat produced no response – the experience of Hansando had been enough to kill that trick stone dead – so Yi changed tactics and arranged for a relay of ships to row in, fire at the Japanese and then withdraw, so that a rolling bombardment was kept up. Yi's report notes that this was indeed successful, and that almost all the Japanese 'pirates', as he perceptively calls them, on the larger vessels were killed or wounded, while many were seen escaping to land. This indicated further danger, because there was every likelihood that the Japanese would take their revenge on the Korean villagers living nearby, so, when only a few Japanese ships were left undamaged, Yi called his fleet off and pulled out to sea to rest for the night. On returning the following morning the surviving Japanese had escaped by ship, leaving the local inhabitants untouched. The report continues:

> We looked over the battleground of the day before, and found that the escaped Japanese had cremated their dead in 12 heaps. There were charred bones and severed hands and legs scattered on the ground, and blood was spattered everywhere, turning the land and sea red …

From the Japanese side the chronicle *Kōrai Funa Senki* gives a concise account of what happened at Angolp'o which tallies with Yi's report on most points of detail, and includes in its description the only specific mention in a Japanese chronicle of the turtle ships:

> However, on the 9th day from the Hour of the Dragon [8.00am], 58 large enemy ships and about 50 small ships came and attacked. Among the large ships were three blind ships [i.e. turtle ships], covered in iron, firing cannons, fire arrows, large (wooden) arrows and so on until the Hour of the Cock [6.00pm].

The same account also adds the interesting information that Kuki Yoshitaka was commanding the fleet from the huge warship, built originally for Hideyoshi, which had become the flagship of the Japanese navy on the outbreak of the Korean War. It was called the *Nihon-maru* (the equivalent of 'HMS *Japan*'), of which more details appear in the *Shima gunki*: 'A three-storey castle was raised up, with a brocade curtain arranged in three layers, and on top was a "Mount Hōrai", and on top of the mountain was a prayer offered to the Ise Shrine.'

The decorative 'Mount Hōrai' (Hōrai is the treasure mountain of Chinese mythology) was a Shintō device with rice heaped up on three sides, and adorned with various sacred objects, so that when 'they blew the conch and advanced upon the Chinamen the sight gave the impression that the Mount Hōrai was floating'. The Koreans were clearly unintimidated by this mystical addition to the Japanese armoury and opened up on the *Nihon-maru* with everything they possessed:

> However, when the fire arrows came flying, we were ready and pulled the charred embers into the sea with ropes, and the ship was not touched. They fired from near at hand with half-bows too, which went through the threefold curtain as far as the second fold, but ended up being stopped at the final layer. They then moved in at close range and when they fired the cannons they destroyed the central side of the *Nihon-maru* for three feet in each direction, but the carpenters had been ordered to prepare for this in advance, and promptly made repairs to keep out the seawater.

The battle of Angolp'o was fought on 16 August, and it was noon of the 17th when Yi's fleet sailed back into the bay in front of Hansan Island that had been the scene of his most complete triumph. There they saw the Japanese who had escaped to that island sitting dazed on the shore, lame and having gone hungry for many days. There were 400 of them, although the Japanese records claim only half this number. By now Yi was receiving reports of Japanese ground troops advancing into Chŏlla Province from the Kŭmsan area, so he withdrew to his base at Yŏsu. The Japanese fugitives then escaped by making rafts out of broken ships' timbers and trees, but the escape of the Japanese prisoners was only a minor blot on an otherwise complete victory. The Korean prime minister, Yu Sŏngnyong, heartened by a further piece of good news on the naval front, pondered on the significance of Hansando in his book *Chingbirok*: 'Japan's original strategy was to combine her ground and naval forces and advance into the western provinces. However, one of her arms was cut off by this single operation. Although Konishi Yukinaga has occupied P'yŏngyang, he can hardly dare to advance because he is isolated.'

At the battle of Ich'i, Kwŏn Yul placed a detached unit as an ambush for the Japanese and routed the invaders.

THE KOREAN GUERRILLA WAR

The second element in the defeat of the Japanese was the Korean resistance on land mounted by three types of warriors. The first were regular troops who had rallied after the initial disasters. Some of their new leaders were serving officers who had received rapid promotion following the death of a general. The second were volunteer armies that went under the general heading of the Ŭibyŏng or 'Righteous Armies'. The final group were the monk soldiers, armies of whom were established in every province very early in the campaign. Theirs was largely a guerrilla war. The activities carried out ranged from straightforward battles and sieges through night raids to the support functions of transporting supplies and building walls. Their operations covered every area where Japanese forces might be challenged, from the Naktong Delta in the south to the Yalu River in the north. For the seven months prior to the arrival of Ming forces in January 1593, an estimated 22,200 irregulars shouldered the burden of resistance together with 84,500 regular soldiers, and made a considerable contribution to the war effort.

Kwak Chae-u as depicted in a painting in the Memorial Museum at Ŭiryŏng. His guerrilla operations gave Korea its first victory of the war.

The first guerrilla leader was Kwak Chae-u, who provided resistance while the regular Korean army still lay shattered. He is remembered today as a romantic and mysterious patriotic hero, appearing from nowhere to defeat the Japanese. Kwak's guerrillas began to prey on the Japanese river boats ferrying newly landed supplies upstream and won an early victory at the battle of Ŭiryŏng. As well as disrupting the Japanese advance, the attacks on the line of the Naktong also provided a similar defence by land to that which Admiral Yi was providing at sea against an incursion westwards into Chŏlla Province.

Within days of Kwak Chae-u raising his volunteer army in Kyŏngsang Province, we also read of a similar force being created over in Chŏlla by a certain Ko Kyŏngmyŏng (1533–92). Ko was 60 years old and a *yangban* (aristocratic scholar) who succeeded in forming an army of 6,000 men, but the brevity of his career, which ended with his death in battle, has prevented him from attaining the legendary status of Kwak Chae-u. His military skills were considerable, but he lacked Kwak's appreciation of the need for

Japanese soldiers beg for mercy as they are overwhelmed by the guerrillas commanded by Kwak Chae-u as depicted on the bas-relief on the side of the plinth of his statue in Taegu.

caution in the face of the Japanese war machine, as shown by his death at the first battle of Kŭmsan.

Kobayakawa Takakage's Sixth Division occupied Kŭmsan, which today is one of the main centres in Korea for the growing of ginseng. It was somewhat isolated, as it lay to the west of the string of communications forts between Pusan and Seoul. With Ko at their head the united Chŏlla army moved in to attack Kŭmsan on 16 August. Resistance was fierce, and the regular troops under Kwak Yŏng on the flank of the Chŏlla army began to waver, so Ko pulled the whole army back. The following day they attacked again, led by 800 men from the Righteous Army, but the Japanese recalled the effect their tactics had produced the previous day and concentrated their attacks on the regular troops. This pressure had the desired effect, and a furious Ko Kyŏngmyŏng saw Kwak Yŏng's troops falling back all round his own gallant band. With a shout to the fleeing Kwak Yŏng of, 'To a defeated general death is the only choice!' he plunged into the enemy and was killed along with his two sons.

The Righteous Army of Ch'ungch'ŏng Province and their leader Cho Hŏn, in company with an army of warrior monks, carried out the next phase of the war. The initiative for inviting Korea's monastic community to join in the struggle against the Japanese seems to have come originally from King Sŏnjo himself. While in exile in Ŭiju the king summoned the monk Hyujŭng and appointed him national leader of all the monk soldiers in Korea. Hyujŏng dispatched a manifesto calling upon monks throughout the land to take arms against the Japanese. 'Alas, the way of heaven is no more', it began. 'The destiny of the land is on the decline. In defiance of heaven and reason

Korean guerrilla operations, 1592

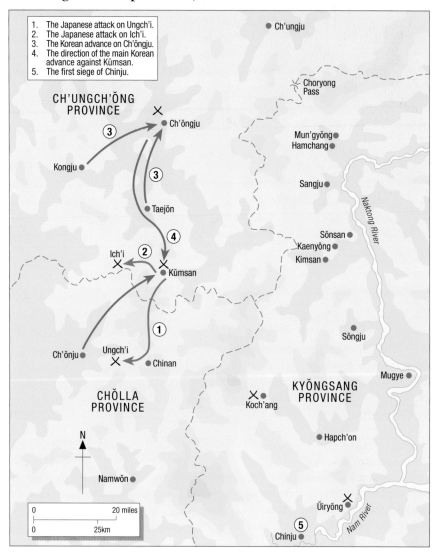

1. The Japanese attack on Ungch'i.
2. The Japanese attack on Ich'i.
3. The Korean advance on Ch'ŏngju.
4. The direction of the main Korean advance against Kŭmsan.
5. The first siege of Chinju.

the cruel foe had the temerity to cross the sea aboard a thousand ships.' The samurai were 'poisonous devils', and 'as virulent as snakes or fierce animals'. He reminded his listeners that one of the Five Secular Precepts, a series of teachings combining Confucianism and Buddhism had been to face battle without retreating. Hyujŏng then called on the monks to 'put on the armour of mercy of Bodhisattvas, hold in hand the treasured sword to fell the devil, wield the lightning bolt of the Eight Deities, and come forward.'

The result of the manifesto was the recruitment of 8,000 monks over the next few months. Some were undoubtedly motivated by patriotism, but others saw it as an opportunity to raise the social status of Buddhist monks, who had suffered from a royal obsession with Confucianism. Although their numbers were small compared with the civilian volunteers their units were cohesive and clearly associated with a particular leader and a particular province. Unfortunately, however, they were not immune from jealousy towards the Righteous Armies, which was to lead to trouble on more than one occasion when a joint operation was being planned.

In Ch'ungch'ŏng Province the driving force in the monk resistance was Abbot Yŭnggyu, who enthusiastically promoted an anti-Japanese movement among his clerical brothers. The first operations in which the monks engaged were guerrilla activities similar to those of their volunteer colleagues, until a major action in September against the Japanese garrison of Ch'ŏngju thrust them into the limelight. Ch'ŏngju was an important transport centre for the Japanese army and also housed an important granary. It was, however, lightly garrisoned, and the Korean volunteers knew it.

On 6 September, Cho Hŏn's Righteous Army of 1,100, together with 1,500 warrior monks and a rearguard of 500, advanced on Ch'ŏngju. The monks attacked the north and east gates, while the volunteers assaulted the west gate. The Japanese quickly drove them off, so Cho Hŏn took up a position on a hill to the west for a second attempt. During the night they lit fires and set up many flags to give the impression of a large host. Fooled completely, the small Japanese garrison planned an immediate evacuation, and the next day Cho Hŏn and his men walked into the castle in triumph. Unfortunately, within days of this considerable Korean victory an argument developed among the leaders over who was to take the credit for it. Different reports were submitted from different viewpoints and relationships deteriorated even further. The tragic result was that a Korean army was at last in a position to take the fight to the enemy, but internal squabbles were threatening to destroy any chance of success.

Thus it was that when a Korean army marched south from Ch'ŏngju to attack Kŭmsan, once again it was a force already doomed by division. The regulars under Yun Sŏngak refused to participate, so the monks and volunteers decided to go ahead without them, but even they were determined to mount two operations independent of each other. The haughty Cho Hŏn planned to launch his attack before the monks, in spite of the fact that the monastic army had now been greatly strengthened by the welcome arrival of another contingent. Cho's incredible plans faced opposition even from within his own depleted ranks, because Kŭmsan was not a lightly garrisoned fort like Ch'ŏngju, but a well defended salient held by 10,000 battle-hardened men under Kobayakawa Takakage. Yun Sŏngak was so opposed to the idea that he went to the length of imprisoning close relatives of the volunteers to

This memorial to the Korean warrior monks who fought during the Japanese invasion is to be found in Seoul.

In this dramatic depiction of guerrilla activity a Japanese patrol is ambushed and pelted with arrows and stones. From *Ehon Taikōki*, an illustrated life of Hideyoshi.

dissuade them from fighting, and even the well-respected Kwŏn Yul lent his weight to the arguments against Cho Hŏn's foolhardy plans.

On 22 September, Cho Hŏn led an army of only 700 volunteer soldiers against 10,000 of the toughest samurai in Korea at the second battle of Kŭmsan. Kobayakawa Takakage soon realized that this isolated force was all that was being sent against him. As night fell the Japanese encircled them and exterminated the entire army, including the reckless Cho Hŏn. Seeing the destruction of his comrade's army, the monk Yŏnggyu felt that he had to follow where Cho Hŏn had led, so over the next three days the monk armies took part in a third battle of Kŭmsan. The result was the same as at the second battle – total annihilation.

A lavish yet very moving memorial shrine called the 'Shrine of the Seven Hundred' now stands on the site of the battles of Kŭmsan. It honours both monk and volunteer alike, and inside one of the halls two dramatic paintings recall the glory of Ch'ŏngju and the disaster of Kŭmsan. Everywhere there is the memory of self-sacrifice and the exhortation for patriotic Koreans to emulate these heroes of old, but nowhere is there any account of the rivalry, pride and selfishness that snatched defeat out of the hands of victory.

Although Cho Hŏn's recklessness lost the battle, it had helped to win the campaign. The fact that Kŭmsan had now suffered three attacks made the Japanese command question whether the Kŭmsan Salient was worth retaining, so Kobayakawa's Sixth Division were pulled back. To the guerrillas this was all that mattered, and this example of what could be achieved encouraged them to carry on with their own campaigns. Another guerrilla leader, Pak Chin, determined to recapture Kyŏngju with a secret weapon. According to *Chingbirok* something was fired over the walls of Kyŏngju and rolled across the courtyard. Not knowing what it was, the 'robbers', as he calls the Japanese garrison, rushed over to examine it. At that moment the object suddenly exploded, sending fragments of iron far and wide and causing over 30 casualties. Such was the alarm it caused that Kyŏngju was evacuated, and the 'robbers' pulled back to the safety of the coastal *wajō* at Sŏsaengp'o.

THE FIRST SIEGE OF CHINJU

The pressure from Korean guerrilla attacks forced Ukita Hideie, the commander of all the Japanese forces, to send reinforcements to Kyŏngsang from Seoul, and towards the end of October the decision was made to capture the Koreans' strongest point in western Kyŏngsang: the town of Chinju, which lay on the Nam River. Chinju was a fortified town with a long high wall that touched the river on its southern side. Between Chinju and the line of the Naktong was Kwak Chae-u's guerrilla territory, and up to that moment in the war the garrison of this strong fortress had never seen a Japanese soldier. Ukita's generals reasoned that if Chinju could be taken then the recaptured castles would fall back into Japanese hands, the guerrillas would lose rear support, and a new road to Chŏlla Province would finally be opened.

The castle of Chinju was under the command of Kim Shimin, who led a garrison of 3,800 men. Kim was a fine general, and was not willing to provide the Japanese with their customary experience of a weak Korean castle defence. Instead he had acquired 170 newly forged Korean harquebuses made to quality standards equivalent to the Japanese ones, and had trained his men in their use. Chinju was the first occasion when these weapons were tried in battle. Kim also had many cannon and a supply of mortars and bombs of the same type that had caused such devastation at Kyŏngju.

The Japanese army crossed the Nam River and approached Chinju from three sides, surprising some Korean stragglers. The *Taikōki* tells us that a certain Jirōza'emon 'took the first head and raised it aloft. The other five men also attacked the enemy army and took some excellent heads.' When the Japanese reached the walls of Chinju, Kim's troops hit back at them with everything in their possession – harquebus balls, bullets, exploding bombs and heavy stones. It was not the reaction Hosokawa and his men had been expecting, so, changing their plans, they made shields out of bamboo and

The fall of Ch'ŏngju to the Righteous Army of Cho Hŏn and the warrior monks under Yŏnggyu is shown here on a painting displayed in the 'Shrine of the Seven Hundred' in Kŭmsan. This was one of the greatest achievements by the irregular forces of Korea.

under the cover of massed volleys of harquebus fire approached close to the walls where long scaling ladders were set up. As the samurai scrambled up the ladders the defenders ignored the bullets and bombarded them with rocks, smashing many ladders to pieces. Meanwhile delayed-action bombs and lumps of stone fell into the mass of soldiers awaiting their turn to fight for the special honour of being first into the castle. The *Taikōki* gives a vivid account of one such endeavour:

> As we try to become *ichiban nori* [first to climb in] they climbed up as in a swarm. Because of this the ladders almost broke, and comrades fell down from

their climb, so they could not use the ladders. Hosokawa Tadaoki's brother Sadaoki was one such, accompanied by foot soldiers on ladders on his right and left, and strictly ordered 'Until I have personally climbed into the castle this ladder is for one person to climb. If anyone else climbs I will take his head!' then he climbed. Because of this the ladder did not break and he got up, and the men who saw him were loud in his praise. Consequently, before very long he placed his hands on the wall, but when he tried to make his entry from within the castle, spears and *naginata* were thrust at him to try to make him fall, and lamentably he fell to the bottom of the moat.

None of the Japanese army was to earn the accolade of *ichiban nori* that day, although many tried, and as the forward troops clawed at Chinju's battlements Japanese labourers behind them were bullied into hurriedly erecting crude siege towers from which harquebuses could shoot down into the courtyard.

For three days this bitter battle, which was unlike anything seen up to that point in the Korean campaign, deposited heaps of Japanese dead in the ditch of Chinju Castle. On the night of 11 November a guerrilla army under Kwak Chae-u arrived to witness the spectacle. It was a pitifully small band to be a relieving force, so Kwak ordered his men to light five pine torches each and hold them aloft as they blew on conch shells and raised a war cry at the tops of their voices. The arrival of a further 500 guerrillas from another direction added to the illusion of a mighty host, then they too were joined by 2,500 more. But the Japanese were not to be diverted from their main objective. Disregarding this newly arrived threat for a short while Hosokawa flung his men into a final attempt to take the castle by storm as he led attacks on the northern and eastern gates during the night of 12 November.

While fighting beside his men on the north gate Commander Kim Shimin received a mortal wound from a bullet in the left of his forehead and fell unconscious to the ground. Seeing this, the Japanese diverted all their troops to the northern side of Chinju's ramparts, trying to gain a handhold on top of the walls, but from the ground below the Koreans swept the walls with arrows and bullets and drove them off. The Chinju garrison were perilously short of ammunition, but just then a Korean detachment arrived by boat up the Nam River bringing welcome supplies of weapons, powder and ball, an event that greatly heartened the garrison. By now all of the Japanese troops had been committed to the assault. They had no rearguard, and were deep inside enemy territory, so to their great chagrin (and the fury of Hideyoshi when he heard about it), the Japanese generals decided to abandon the siege of Chinju. It was a deep embarrassment. The Korean revival – the second element in the resistance against Japan – had produced results as inspiring as Yi Sunsin's naval victories.

The rapidity of the Japanese advance and the enormity of the Korean collapse initially made the Ming suspicious that the Koreans were in league with the invaders. At the conference depicted here Yu Sŏngnyong convinced the Chinese otherwise. From *Ehon Taikōki*, an illustrated life of Hideyoshi.

THE CHINESE LIBERATION OF KOREA

Taking an overview of the Korean campaign, while the naval victories and the guerrilla raids were very important in preventing the Japanese from advancing, it was the intervention of Ming China that threw the entire operation into reverse. From the time of the Chinese recapture of P'yŏngyang in February 1593 the Japanese army's movements were those of retreat.

The Chinese intervention may have been long in coming, but it was formidable in its eventual execution. The genuine desire by the Chinese to help Korea had always been somewhat outweighed by their outrage at Japan's challenge to the Ming's authority on continental East Asia. That affront alone required a military response, but the continuing Ningxia situation had meant that it was much delayed. The first move by the Chinese was not carried out until late August 1592 and comes across as little more than a token gesture because an army of only 3,000 troops was ordered to retake P'yŏngyang. Their commander Zu Chengxun nevertheless felt very confident that he had sufficient resources to fulfil his task. He was after all an experienced general who had fought the Mongols and the Jurchens and had nothing but contempt for the Japanese.

The exact layout of P'yŏngyang's defences will be described later in the account of the successful operation in 1593; for now it is sufficient to note

The temple of Yŏngmyŏngsa lay at the foot of Mount Moranbong, and was to experience some very fierce action during the siege of P'yŏngyang.

that Zu Chengxun's attempt proved to be a very short-lived affair. Boasting that he had once defeated 100,000 Jurchens with 3,000 horsemen, the supremely confident general took advantage of a heavy rainstorm to attack P'yŏngyang at dawn on 23 August. He seems to have taken Konishi Yukinaga completely by surprise because Yoshino Jingoza'emon, whose *Chōsen ki* (*Korea Diary*) provides a valuable eyewitness account, writes of 'the enemy entering in secret'. Most of the Japanese army did not have time to put on their armour and just seized whatever weapons lay to hand as the Chinese flung themselves against the walls. Matsuura Shigenobu was but one of the First Division's commanders who became personally engaged in combat, receiving an arrow through his leg.

Zu Chengxun's success in entering P'yŏngyang by storm was to prove his undoing. When the Japanese realized that they outnumbered the attacking army by six to one they allowed the Liaodong troops to spread freely into the narrow streets of the walled city. Soon what had been a hammer blow action against one section of the wall rapidly diffused into hundreds of ineffective skirmishes by small groups of isolated Chinese soldiers who could be picked off at will by the Japanese harquebuses. A retreat was called, so the survivors were allowed to flood out of the opened gates. Once they were in the open and hindered by the deep mud the mounted samurai cut them down in their dozens. The Chinese mobile corps commander, Shi Ru, was killed, and Zu Chengxun barely escaped with his life.

The Japanese defenders of P'yŏngyang, as depicted on a Chinese painted screen in the Hizen-Nagoya Castle Museum. Their weapons include harquebuses and *naginata*.

The defeat of the first Chinese expeditionary force produced mixed reactions among the Japanese commanders. There was certainly an initial feeling of elation at having beaten off a Ming army, and as reinforcements from Japan were expected to arrive any day this dramatic confirmation of Japan's superiority added to their readiness to press on for the Yalu River. But the days soon grew into months and no reinforcements arrived. News was received that guerrillas were harassing Japanese communications by land while Admiral Yi was completely severing them by sea, and the feeling also grew that the Chinese would return in far greater numbers. It was a concern shared at the highest level of the Japanese command, and Konishi Yukinaga journeyed to Seoul for a conference with Ukita Hideie. The gloomy conclusion they reached was that when P'yŏngyang was attacked again it might fall because it was now so isolated.

The decisive Ming advance came with the turning of the year. The crushing of the Ningxia revolt finally gave the Chinese the opportunity they needed to convince the Japanese that their fears of the mighty Ming were well grounded. Li Rusong, the hero of Ningxia, was made commander of the Korean expeditionary force, and set off to relieve P'yŏngyang with a recent siege success under his belt. Li was a much more patient character than his predecessor, and showed that he was capable of learning from Zu Chengxun's mistakes. His first decision was not to risk another attack in summer but to wait until the bitter Korean winter had frozen the ground solid so that his artillery train could be moved with ease. During the autumn his subordinate commanders received training at Shanhaiguan on the Great Wall, and eventually 30,000 men and three months' supply of food had been assembled in Liaodong. The target number was 75,000, although the Ming hierarchy believed that 100,000 were actually needed if the task was to be accomplished quickly. With only 75,000, it was feared, Li Rusong would need a year to drive the Japanese out, but less than half that number had been assembled. They were nevertheless well supplied with weapons and winter clothing, and enough silver had been released from the Ming defence budget to provide 200 more cannon.

On 5 January 1593, Wu Weizhong led an advance guard across the Yalu River. It consisted of 3,000 men, and two more battalions of 2,000 each followed them. They waited for Li Rusong with the main body at Ŭiju, where King Sŏnjo of Korea greeted the Chinese as saviours. He was accompanied by his prime minister, Yu Sŏngnyong, who provided maps of the area and brought the Chinese up to date on the existing military situation. The Chinese army was then arranged into three divisions. Li Rubo, Li Rusong's younger brother, commanded the left wing, Yang Yuan commanded the centre while Zhang Shijue commanded the right. A rapid advance from Ŭiju followed that left their horses sweating heavily in spite of the cold.

Unlike his predecessor, Li Rusong made good use of advanced scouts and soon flushed out a Japanese advance party, from whom five were killed and three captured. Another skirmish followed in a forest to the north of P'yŏngyang until, on 5 February 1593, Li Rusong drew up his ranks outside the city. Early next morning Konishi Yukinaga offered to talk terms with Li Rubo within P'yŏngyang, but the cautious Li Rubo feared a trap and refused. That night his camp was attacked by a Japanese sortie but his alert guards warned him and the Japanese were driven back to the accompaniment of fire arrows. A false retreat was ordered, and some Japanese were foolish enough to follow the Chinese lead and became ambushed themselves.

The task facing the Chinese was a considerable one, because P'yŏngyang enjoyed a naturally strong position and was defended by some of Korea's more formidable walls. They enclosed an area that was largely flat apart from Mount Changwang (40m) in the south-west of the walled city. The Taedong

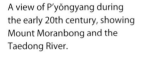

A view of P'yŏngyang during the early 20th century, showing Mount Moranbong and the Taedong River.

The first fighting during the Chinese recapture of P'yŏngyang was an attempt to control Mount Moranbong, where Konishi Yukinaga established his command post. It lay just to the north of the city proper and dominated the river. Here we see Konishi Yukinaga defending the so-called Tree Peony Pavilion on its summit. From *Ehon Taikōki*, an illustrated life of Hideyoshi.

River protected the city to the east and had acted as a moat when the Japanese attacked in 1592, but in January 1593 the Taedong was of less importance than the narrower Pot'ong River that flowed on the other side of the city and provided defence against an attack from the north-west. The city walls of P'yŏngyang formed a crude elongated triangle lying between the Pot'ong and Taedong rivers, within which were six gates. The Changgyŏng and Taedong gates gave access to the river on the east. The Ch'ilsŏng (Seven Stars) Gate allowed access to the north-west. From there the wall continued south and touched the Pot'ong River on its western side where lay the Pot'ong Gate. In the south wall were the Chŏngyang Gate and the Hangu Gate. Leaving the Taedong River gates lightly defended, each of the four landward main gates of the city was defended by 2,000 Japanese troops. There are no records of which gates were assigned to which commanders, but we do know that P'yŏngyang was defended solely by the First Division who had landed so triumphantly in Pusan seven months earlier. Most of the remainder of the 15,000 soldiers under Konishi Yukinaga's overall command were within the walls and ready to be moved wherever they were needed, although a small number may have been stationed on Nŭngna Island in the middle of the Taedong River as a rearguard to cover the crossing points in case of a retreat. All Korean civilians in the city had been evacuated.

One vital sector in P'yŏngyang's defences, however, lay just to the north of the city proper. This was Mount Moranbong, which dominated the area and was physically included in the city's defensive perimeter by means of walls that ran up its slopes and were furnished with fortified gates. In peacetime Mount Moranbong was a popular place from which to enjoy the attractive view of the river over the tree peonies on its slopes. The picturesquely named Choesung Pavilion (Tree Peony Pavilion or Botandai in the Japanese chronicles) on its summit at 70m above sea level provided the command post for Konishi Yukinaga and 2,000 bodyguard troops, and was to see some of the fiercest fighting of the forthcoming battle. A Buddhist temple, the Yŏngmyŏngsa, lay on the mountain's southern side.

OPPOSING FORCES

Japanese
1. Konishi Yukinaga
2. Sō Yoshitomo
3. Reserves
4. Omura Yoshiaki
5. Arima Harunobu
6. Gotō Sumiharu

Korean
A. Yi Il
B. Kim Ŭngsŏ
C. Hyujŏng

Chinese
D. Li Rusong
E. Li Rubo
F. Wu Weizhong
G. Yang Yuan
H. Zhang Shijue
I. Zu Chengxun

MT MORANBONG

CHOESUNG PAVILIO (BOTANDAI)

YŎNGMYŎN TEMPLE

INNER CITADE

CH'ILSŎNG GATE

POT'ONG RIVER

xxxx
LI RUSONG

▼ EVENTS

1 5 February Li Rusong establishes strong siege lines round P'yŏngyang. He has benefited from the previous experience of the Chinese general Zu Chengxun who stormed the city and was led into a trap.

2 6 February Dawn: The first Chinese advance takes place. This is an operation to capture Mount Moranbong, which protects P'yŏngyang from the north. Korean warrior monks under Hyujŏng are allowed to spearhead the attack on Moranbong

3 Afternoon: The Japanese resistance proves to be very fierce. Chinese troops under Wu Weizhong assist the Koreans on Moranbong by advancing from the west.

4 Late afternoon: The Japanese commander Konishi Yukinaga is completely surrounded by the Chinese and Korean attack and has to be rescued by Sō Yoshitomo, who breaks through from the city to allow the Japanese survivors to regroup.

5 Evening: Mount Moranbong is finally abandoned by the Japanese, who evacuate the position and take up stations in the Inner Citadel of P'yŏngyang.

6 7 February: Li Rusong plans an assault from several directions. An artillery bombardment of P'yŏngyang begins. The fire is directed against the walls and the gates to soften up the Japanese positions ready for the Chinese attack

7 8 February: The main assault by the Chinese and Korean armies takes place; the Ch'ilsŏng Gate is the first Japanese position to be destroyed. Chinese troops enter the city and street fighting begins.

8 Afternoon: All the gates of P'yŏngyang have now been captured; the Japanese begin to abandon the outer city areas and withdraw to the Inner Citadel for a last stand.

9 Late afternoon: Before retreating to the Inner Citadel Konishi Yukinaga leads a brave sortie out against some Korean troops. They turn out to be Chinese troops disguised as Koreans. The final Japanese units pull back and enter the Inner Citadel.

10 Evening: The Chinese and Koreans attack the Inner Citadel, which holds out because of heavy and deadly Japanese harquebus fire.

11 Night: Konishi Yukinaga holds a council of war and the decision to abandon P'yŏngyang is made. Konishi Yukinaga leads a secret evacuation of P'yŏngyang. The Japanese cross the river and head for the next communications fort.

THE CHINESE RECAPTURE P'YŎNGYANG, 1593

Li Rusong forces the Japanese First Division under Konishi Yukinaga back across the Taedung River

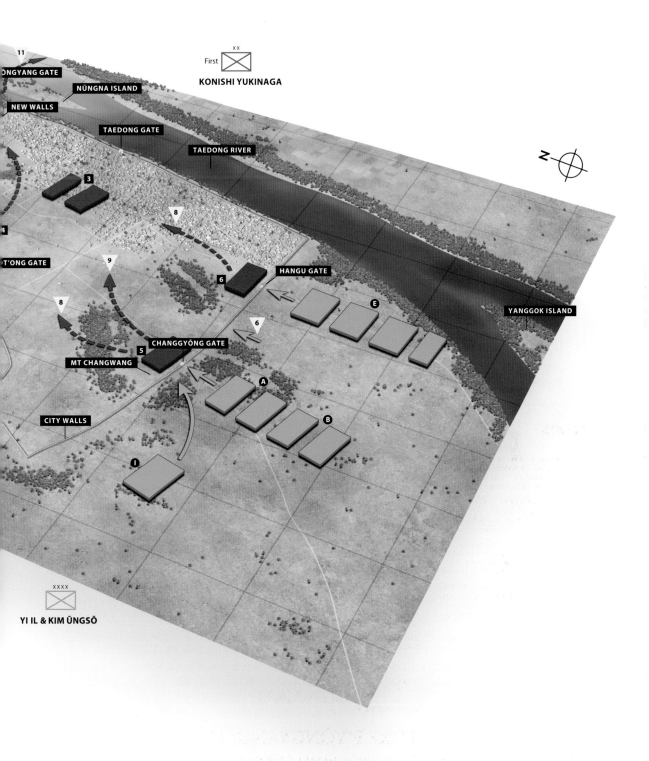

11

ŎNGYANG GATE

NŬNGNA ISLAND

NEW WALLS

First ⊠ ××
KONISHI YUKINAGA

TAEDONG GATE

TAEDONG RIVER

N

3

8

4

T'ONG GATE

9

8

6

HANGU GATE

E

6

CHANGGYŎNG GATE

5

MT CHANGWANG

A

B

YANGGOK ISLAND

CITY WALLS

I

××××
⊠
YI IL & KIM ŬNGSŎ

The Japanese had also constructed an inner defensive citadel within the tight triangle of the walls in the north-eastern section of the city, but because of the shortage of time and a deep distrust of Korean military architecture that the experience of the past months had done little to dispel, this was done by creating Japanese-style earthworks rather than building more stone walls. The embankments were reinforced with trenches and palisades that would allow a clear field of fire for the defenders and would also provide absorbency for the cannon balls that were likely to be fired against them by the Chinese field artillery. Clever use was also made of discarded swords and daggers, because Yu Sŏngnyong noted that 'The spears and swords that the Japanese had set up on the battlements, pointed at the Chinese soldiers, looked like the needles of a porcupine.'

Li Rusong's 43,000-strong army had now been swollen by an additional 10,000 Korean troops under Yi Il and Kim Ŭngsŏ, some regulars, some volunteers and 5,000 warrior monks. Korean records also tell of the presence of over 40,000 Jurchens under the banner of Nurhaci. If this is correct it demonstrates how ineffective Katō Kiyomasa's north-eastern campaign had been, but Chinese accounts do not mention any Jurchens and instead record considerable disappointment that only half the number of troops they wanted had been assembled. Li Rusong was also concerned about the lack of discipline among his troops, and rigorously weeded out 400 men whom he considered to be too old or too weak to fight. On a brighter note supplies continued to arrive, so Li could count on enough food for four months. His artillery train was also most impressive. Li Rusong appreciated that the Japanese had superiority in hand-held firearms, but dismissed them with the words, 'Japanese weapons have a range of a few hundred paces, while my great cannon have a range of five to six *li* [2.4km]. How can we not be victorious?'

Li Rusong set up his headquarters on high ground to the west of the Pot'ong River with 9,000 men, and deployed 10,000 Chinese troops under Zhang Shijue against the Ch'ilsŏng Gate and 11,000 under Yang Yuan against the Pot'ong Gate. A further 10,000 Chinese under Li Rubo faced the Hangu Gate, while 8,000 Koreans under Yi Il and Kim Ŭngsŏ were ordered to attack

Here we see the Chinese army breaking into the Ch'ilsŏng Gate with the Japanese defenders fleeing back inside. From *Ehon Taikōki*, an illustrated life of Hideyoshi.

the Chŏngyang Gate. Li's overall plan was to surround P'yŏngyang with his artillery and open fire on to the city from four directions. This would create chaos among the defenders and provide a cloud of smoke under which the Chinese could advance, with the initial objective being the strategic Mount Moranbong. His cannon were therefore distributed evenly round the city and carefully guarded. To ensure that discipline was enforced Li gave orders that anyone fleeing from the attack should be beheaded. Once the city was entered the rule was that ordinary Japanese soldiers were to be killed outright while senior officers should be captured alive. On being driven out of the city any fleeing Japanese who did not then drown in the Taedong River were to be cut down without any mercy.

After a botched attempt to assassinate Konishi Yukinaga by inviting him to peace talks and laying an ambush, the conventional assault began. Three thousand Korean warrior monks, whose fighting qualities were greatly respected by Li Rusong, were allocated to attack Konishi Yukinaga on Mount Moranbong. The Korean monk army was under the command of Hyujŏng, the leader who had first called the religious contingent to arms and, on 6 February 1593, he led his men up the steep northern slopes in the face of fierce harquebus fire to begin the battle for P'yŏngyang. There were hundreds of casualties, but the monks persevered, and received support rather late in the day from a Chinese unit under Wu Weizhong, whose unit began scaling the western slopes. Wu Weizhong received a bullet in his chest. There was soon a real danger that Konishi Yukinaga would be isolated from his main army and be killed, but Sō Yoshitomo, who was determined to die overwhelmed by impossible odds like the noble samurai of old, led a counterattack and rescued him.

The battle for Mount Moranbong continued for two days. Matsuura Shigenobu appears to have been the last Japanese commander to leave, and on that second day Li Rusong ordered a general assault on the rest of the city. The Chinese cannon boomed out from all directions while incendiary bombs and fire arrows were loosed over the walls and set many buildings ablaze. The mountains echoed to the cannon's roar, and even the surrounding

Chinese soldiers wielding spears and halberds attack P'yŏngyang under the protection of cannon fire, as depicted on a Chinese painted screen in the Hizen-Nagoya Castle Museum

forest caught fire. With the sound of the first cannon providing the signal to advance, the Chinese with Li Rusong at their head advanced in a probing assault to be met by a withering harquebus fire from the walls topped with sword blades, from where the Japanese thrust out long spears, dropped rocks, loosed arrows and poured boiling water. One Ming officer had his feet crushed by a falling rock. Smoke began to obscure the scene, and eyewitnesses of the fighting described how the Chinese corpses piled up so densely outside the walls that they made a ramp up which their comrades clambered.

Li Rusong was so involved in the fighting for the walls that his horse was shot dead beneath him. To stiffen his men's resolve he publicly killed a fleeing Chinese soldier and offered 5,000 ounces of silver to the first man to get over the wall. Siege ladders on wheeled carts, the famous 'cloud ladders' of Chinese siegecraft, helped the process along, and Luo Shangzhi from Zhejiang Province became one of the first to break in, wielding his huge halberd like an ancient Chinese war god. With such determination, and at a heavy cost in casualties, all the landward gates were taken. Yang Yuan broke through the Pot'ong Gate as a bloody street fight began. The monk survivors of the attack on Mount Moranbong and Wu Weizhong's Chinese troops joined Zhang Shijue to fight their way in through the Ch'ilsŏng Gate where all defences had been destroyed by cannon fire. Spurred on by Li Rusong's promises of reward, heads, armour and clothing were taken from corpses to provide the necessary evidence that the victim was a high-ranking Japanese officer.

Under intense Chinese pressure the Japanese were driven back all along the line, and the entire length of the city walls was finally evacuated for the inner citadel. The Chinese who had broken through surged forwards and caught sight of the crude defences of the makeshift Japanese castle, which drew scorn from the Ming officers. They compared the mounds of earth unfavourably with their own elegant Great Wall of China. These simple defences were more like the earthen walls thrown up by the barbarous Jurchens, but that was before these Chinese officers had experienced the volleys of Japanese bullets that were to be discharged from behind them. Yu Sŏngnyong refers to the surprise they presented to them in *Chingbirok*: 'The enemy built clay walls with holes on top of their fortress, which looked like a beehive. They fired their muskets through those holes as much as they could, and as a result, a number of Chinese soldiers were wounded.'

The Chinese and Korean ranks were so tightly packed that the volleys of harquebus balls caused considerable casualties. Many retreated out of the Ch'ilsŏng Gate, and at some point Konishi Yukinaga bravely led his men out to break out from the inner citadel but was driven back by cannon fire. As his troops swung round they encountered what they believed were Korean soldiers. They turned out to be Chinese disguised as Koreans under the former attacker of P'yŏngyang, Zu Chengxun, a revelation that is said to have created panic.

By now the winter's night was drawing on, and as Li Rusong had his enemy cornered he was loath to provoke any more desperate sallies, so he called off his men to rest until morning. That night Konishi Yukinaga made the decision to retreat. Under cover of darkness, the entire Japanese garrison took advantage of the frozen surface of the Taedong River, slipped out of Changgyŏng Gate and evacuated the city across Nŭnga Island without either the Chinese or Korean armies knowing anything about it. As Yoshino Jingoza'emon tells us:

> There was hardly a gap between the dead bodies that filled the surroundings of Matsuyama Castle [Mount Moranbong]. Finally, when we had repulsed the enemy, they burned the food storehouses in several places, so there was now no food. On the night of the seventh day we evacuated the castle, and made our escape. Wounded men were abandoned, while those who were not wounded but simply exhausted crawled almost prostrate along the road.

Konishi Yukinaga's retreat to Seoul took nine painful days. The first refuge for this ragged, tired, frozen and wounded army was P'ungsan, the nearest of the communications forts that lay back along the line towards Seoul, held by Otomo Yoshimune of the Third Division. But an unpleasant surprise lay in store for Konishi's men, because to their astonishment P'ungsan had been abandoned. Patrols sent out by Otomo had reported to him that Konishi was under attack and that both fields and mountains were filled with enemy soldiers. Otomo Yoshimune's conclusion was that Konishi had probably been defeated already by the time his scouts had ridden back. No relief march was conceivable with his tiny garrison, nor could they withstand the huge force that must be bearing down upon them, so Otomo decided to burn P'ungsan and retreat to Seoul. Yoshino puts into words the hardship this extraordinary decision caused to the wounded and frostbitten survivors of Konishi's army:

> Because it is a cold country, there is ice and deep snow, and hands and feet are burned by the snow, and this gives rise to frostbite which make them swell up. The only clothes they had were the garments worn under their armour, and even men who were normally gallant resembled scarecrows on the mountains and fields because of their fatigue, and were indistinguishable from the dead.

A diary kept by a member of the Yoshimi family adds snow-blindness to the list of afflictions from which the wounded men were suffering. These unfortunates were now faced with a further day's march through the wind and snow to the next fort, but a samurai's cowardice in the face of an enemy could not easily be forgiven. Otomo's family, one of the oldest and noblest in Kyūshū, and one of the first and greatest of the Christian *daimyō*, was now disgraced irreparably and forever.

THE SIEGE OF HAENGJU

The fall of P'yŏngyang was the turning point in the first invasion. The retreat that Konishi Yukinaga had begun when he evacuated the city through its eastern gates was to end at Pusan a few months later with very little delay or counteroffensive. Much is made in the Japanese accounts of their rearguard victory at Pyŏkjeyek to the north of Seoul, which proved to be the biggest land battle of the war and resulted in the triumphant Li Rusong being driven

Konishi Yukinaga leads the evacuation of P'yŏngyang out of the Changgyŏng Gate and across the frozen Taedong River. From *Ehon Taikōki*, an illustrated life of Hideyoshi.

back northwards in disgrace. But in spite of the heavy Chinese losses it did nothing to change the overall strategy, and the retreat from Seoul was delayed by only a few days. Pyŏkjeyek was nevertheless a numerical victory for the Japanese. In the fierce hand-to-hand fighting the razor-sharp edges of the Japanese blades cut deep into the heavy coats of the Chinese, while Japanese foot soldiers tugged mounted men from the backs of their horses using the short cross blades on their spears. Li Rusong was unhorsed in the thick of the fighting, so Li Yousheng used his own body to provide a shield for his commander, who was rescued when his brothers attacked. The brave subordinate general's sacrifice had not been made in vain, because it enabled Li Rusong to escape from the field.

Attention then shifted to the fortress of Haengju on a hill 13km northwest of Seoul. It overlooked the Han River and covered all approaches down to the capital. On hearing of the Chinese advance against Seoul, Chŏlla Province's skilled general Kwŏn Yul took over this dilapidated castle which possessed steep cliffs on the river side and abrupt slopes in all other directions. Kwŏn Yul's 2,300 men, including a monk contingent, strengthened Haengju's fortifications with ditches and palisades and waited for the opportunity to join the Chinese attack on Seoul.

The battle of Pyŏkjeyek, of course, meant that Kwŏn Yul was waiting in vain, and having won that battle so decisively Ukita Hideie decided to make Haengju his next triumph. At dawn on 14 March, Ukita led a massive 30,000-strong Japanese army out of Seoul to crush the minor annoyance. Konishi Yukinaga and Kobayakawa Takakage are two of the famous names that took part. The attack began about 6.00am with little overall plan, just a steady advance up the steep slopes of Haengju from all directions. But the Koreans were waiting for them. Dug in behind earthworks and palisades they replied with bows, harquebuses, delayed-action mortar bombs, rocks and tree trunks. Pride of place in the Haengju armoury, however, was a substantial number of the curious armoured artillery vehicles called *hwach'a* (fire wagons). A *hwach'a* consisted of a wooden cart pushed by two men on level ground, or four on steep ground. On top of the cart was mounted one of two varieties of a honeycomb-like framework from which either 100 steel-tipped rockets or 200 thin arrows shot from gun tubes could be discharged at once. Timing was of course crucial, because a *hwach'a* could not be easily reloaded, but the Japanese attack at Haengju was delivered in the form of dense formations of men marching slowly up a steep slope, so conditions could hardly have been better.

Haengju is regarded, with Hansando and the first battle of Chinju, as one of the three great Korean victories of the war. In an action that had passed into legend even the women of the garrison played their part, carrying stones to the front line in their aprons and their skirts. In spite of the hail of missiles the overwhelming superiority in numbers of the Japanese forced Kwŏn Yul's troops back onto their second line of defence, but they went no farther. Nine attacks in all were made against Haengju, and each was beaten off for a total Japanese casualty list that Korean sources claim may have reached 10,000 dead or wounded. After the battle, notes Yi Sŏngnyong in *Chingbirok*, 'Kwŏn Yul ordered his soldiers to gather the dead bodies of the enemy and vent their anger by tearing them apart and hanging them on the branches of the trees.'

Ukita Hideie, who was appointed Supreme Commander following the successful landing. He was based in Seoul and led the attack on Haengju. (From a hanging scroll in Okayama Castle, reproduced by kind permission)

The result of the Haengju debacle was that within a space of less than 20 days the Japanese had gained one tremendous victory and suffered one humiliating defeat, with the inevitable result that the military effects of each cancelled the other out. The Chinese army had withdrawn, but they were expected to return, and the Korean position was stronger than ever after the engagement at Haengju. The despondent Chinese general Li Rusong resolved to return to the fray when he heard of the triumph at Haengju, and Chinese troops began to move south towards Seoul once again.

Within the capital were scenes of misery and chaos. A mere 11 months had passed since over 150,000 Japanese troops had landed in Korea. Now the best estimate of the army's strength was 53,000 men. Death and wounds from numerous battles, sieges, frostbite, guerrilla raids and typhoid fever had taken a huge toll, and the chronicler noted how the common soldiers had suffered frostbite and snow-blindness, and one or two had even been eaten by tigers while on sentry duty.

To the background of an eerie truce, which was frequently broken by both sides, the Japanese army evacuated Seoul and headed south, its vanguard crossing the Naktong River at the end of May, and finally pulled their rearguard into the safety of Pusan in early June. The Chinese army officially liberated Seoul on 19 May. Yu Sŏngnyong described the ghastly scene in *Chingbirok*:

> The moment I entered the castle, I counted the number of survivors among the citizens, who totalled only one out of every hundred. Yet they looked like ghosts, betraying their great sufferings from hunger and fatigue. The corpses of both men and horses were exposed under the extreme heat of the season, producing an unbearable stench which filled the streets of the city. I passed

KWŎN YUL DEFENDS HAENGJU AGAINST THE JAPANESE ATTACK 1593 (pp. 64–65)

Haengju was a small *sansŏng* (mountain fortress) to the north of Seoul and was the site of one of the most important Korean victories during the invasion. As the Japanese retreated towards Seoul after the fall of P'yŏngyang Korea's ablest general, Kwŏn Yul, reinforced Haengju and waited to join the Chinese advance on the capital. However, because the battle of Pyŏkjeyek had stalled the Chinese advance the Japanese were newly confident. Seeing this mountain fortress in their way, Haengju came under attack from Ukita Hideie.

In this plate we see the desperate defence of Haengju, which shows good use of the mountain location and the deployment of Korean military skills at their finest. To the rear General Kwŏn Yul **(1)** directs the operations from on horseback accompanied by his standard-bearer. The brunt of the attack is being borne at the edge of the plateau, which has been cleared to provide a clear field of fire and reinforced with stakes and a stone wall **(2)**. Rocks are thrown down onto the advancing Japanese, the stone missiles being brought to the defenders by women carrying the projectiles in their aprons, a famous feature of the legendary

defence. Good use is also made of the *hwach'a* **(3)**, the dramatic rocket-firing carts. Timing was of course crucial, and the defenders of Haengju have clearly waited until a sizeable group of Japanese are in close range. As the assault party, flying from their armour blue flags bearing the *mon* (badge) of Ukita Hideie **(4)**, reach the wall the *hwach'a* is fired with a deafening roar, and the rockets tipped with arrowheads fly down into the midst of the Japanese. The Korean standing next to the cart covers his ears. A further supply of rockets is cautiously brought up, and in the middle of the picture we see a *hwach'a* being reloaded from a fresh salvo **(5)**. Otherwise the Koreans use harquebuses, bows and arrows, swords and tridents. The successful defence of Haengju effectively neutralized the new wave of optimism that the Japanese had after Pyŏkjeyek, and it was not long before Seoul was evacuated for good. The plate is based on an oil painting in the Memorial Shrine to Kwŏn Yul and the defenders of Haengju that has been erected on the summit of the mountain overlooking the Han River to the north of Seoul.

Kwŏn Yul defending Haengju, from the bas-relief on the monument on the site of the battle. The *hwach'a* (rocket wagons) and the women bringing stones in their aprons are well illustrated.

the residential districts, both public and private, only to find remnants of complete destruction. Also gone were the ancestral shrines of the royal family, the court palaces, government offices, office buildings and various schools. No trace of the old grandeur could be seen.

THE SECOND SIEGE OF CHINJU

During the retreat to the coast the Japanese gained one last victory as an act of revenge, because the failure by the Japanese army to capture Chinju in November 1592 appears to have infuriated Hideyoshi more than any other defeat suffered at Korean hands. The debacle at Haengju could be seen to have been offset by the great victory at Pyŏkjeyek, while Hansando had happened as victories on land were being gained elsewhere. Chinju stood alone as a Japanese humiliation. It was a fortress apparently no different from any that had fallen so easily to Japanese attack during those triumphant first months of the march on Seoul, and, in view of the great strength of the Japanese forces that had been brought against it, the failure to take it was a disgrace that had to be expunged. Ukita Hideie committed a total of over 90,000 troops to the Chinju campaign, the largest Japanese force mobilized for a single operation in the entire war. At least half of these were reinforcements brought over from Japan and placed under generals who had already fought from one end of Korea to the other.

The Korean commanders learned of the new Japanese advance, but not knowing what might be the Japanese objective, Kwŏn Yul headed for Chŏnju while Kim Ch'ŏnil entered Chinju, and took charge of its defences against a possible attack. Chinju had a permanent garrison of 4,000, which soon grew to a possible 60,000 through the arrival of guerrillas, volunteers and many civilians, including women and children, who packed themselves into its walls. Chinju was protected to the south by cliffs overlooking the Nam River, and the long perimeter walls with towers and gateways that stretched round the city on the other three sides made it look like a miniature version of P'yŏngyang. Like P'yŏngyang, Chinju had a bower for viewing the river, the

RIGHT
The women at Haengju
bringing stones in their
aprons to the defenders of the
mountain fortress, from the
bas-relief on the monument
on the site of the battle.

BELOW
A view of Chinju Castle today,
looking along the line of the
Nam River.

Ch'oksŏngnu Pavilion, which looked over the Nam River on the castle's southern side. Some Chinese troops, who optimistically claimed to be the vanguard of a great force that was approaching from the north, entered the castle amidst great rejoicing.

On 20 July, the Japanese vanguard was observed to be constructing bamboo bundles and setting up wooden shields in sight of the walls of Chinju. To the west was Konishi Yukinaga with 26,000 men. To the north was Katō Kiyomasa with 25,000 troops, while to the east was Ukita Hideie in command of a further 17,000. Beyond them was a further ring of Japanese soldiers whose eyes were turned as much in the direction of a possible Chinese advance as to the castle itself. On the hills to the north-west stood Kobayakawa Takakage with 8,700 men, while Mōri Hidemoto and 13,000 troops covered the north and east. Finally, across the Nam to the south was Kikkawa Hiroie, with an unrecorded number of troops, ready to cut off any Korean guerrillas coming from that direction.

The Chinju garrison had tried to augment their defences by cutting a moat from the stream that fed the Nam River to the north to flood part of the outer ditch to make a wet moat, but on the first day of the Japanese attack on 21 July advance troops broke the edges of the dyke and drained off the water. As they proceeded to fill the ditch with rocks, earth and brushwood, assault parties drew steadily nearer to the walls under cover of shields made from bamboo bundles, some of which may have been mounted on a wheeled framework. The Koreans replied with harquebuses, cannon balls and fire arrows, shattering or burning the bamboo defences. Two days later the Japanese tried the same technique that had been used during the first siege of Chinju by erecting static siege towers, to which the Koreans responded by

The decisive moment in the siege of Chinju was the collapse of a section of the outer wall, brought about by undermining the foundations under the protection of turtle shell wagons, fortified mobile shelters. A fortuitous rainstorm completed the work. From *Ehon Taikōki*, an illustrated life of Hideyoshi.

increasing the defences within the castle and firing back. 'His Lordship [Kim Ch'ŏnil] … secretly fired the cannons', says a Korean account. 'The cannon balls hit the lines, and the enemy generals fell to the ground.' At about this time a local Righteous Army arrived in support, but was driven off by the Japanese rearguard.

On 25 July, Ukita Hideie sent a message into the castle calling upon Kim Ch'ŏnil to surrender and arguing that if one general submitted then 10,000 peasants' lives would be saved, but the request drew no response. Instead the inspiring figure of Kim Ch'ŏnil urged his men to fight to the last:

> His Lordship had an inherent weakness in his legs and could not walk, so in the castle he travelled in a shoulder palanquin, but took little rest by day or night. He prepared rice gruel with his own hands, and made sure that the members of the garrison ate it. All the soldiers were inspired, and pledged themselves to the death.

It was now time for a major Japanese assault to be led by 'tortoise shell wagons', which were stout wooden 'sows' on wheels that were pushed up to the edge of the walls. Under the protection of the wagons' boarded roofs, foundation stones would be dug out of the ramparts, leading to the collapse of a section. One account tells us:

> At Kuroda Nagamasa's duty station they filled up almost the whole width by working day and night. This was done by throwing grass into the ditch to make a flat surface. They tried to attack, but from inside the castle pine torches were thrown that set the grass alight. The soldiers inside the tortoise wagons were also burned and retreated.

The burning of the wagons, which was done by the simple expedient of dropping bundles of combustible material soaked in oil or fat from the battlements, drove off this assault. Undaunted, Katō Kiyomasa ordered other wagons to be prepared and had their roofs covered with ox hides for fire prevention. On 27 July a new attack began that concentrated on the wall's cornerstones in the north-east, and a fortuitous rainstorm helped dislodge the foundations. The customary rush to claim the distinction of being first into the fortress commenced as soon as the stones in the wall began to slide, with samurai pushing each other out of the way. Seeing that Gotō Mototsugu, one of Kuroda's retainers, was likely to be the first to climb in, Katō's standard-bearer Iida Kakubei threw the great Nichiren flag over the wall to claim his place.

By this time the garrison were so short of weapons and ammunition that they were fighting with wooden sticks, but at least one senior defender still had a sword. This was General Sŏ Yewŏn. When the Japanese broke in he opened one of the gates and sallied out twice to fight an individual combat with Okamoto Gonojō, a retainer of Kikkawa Hiroie. On the second occasion, however, Okamoto pursued him back to the gate and forced his way into the courtyard, where the injured and exhausted Sŏ was sitting on the stump of a large tree. Pausing for breath, Okamoto unsheathed his sword, leapt upon him and struck off his head. To one side of this place was the edge of a steep cliff, and Sŏ's head tumbled down into the grass beneath. As it was unthinkable for a noble samurai to lose such a prized head a search was made of the riverbank until it was found.

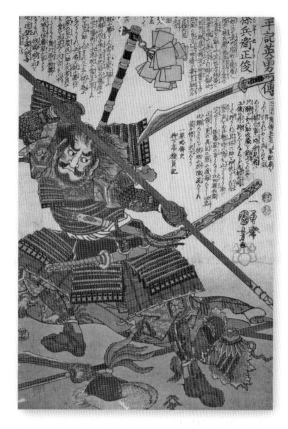

Keyamura Rokunosuke, also known as Kida Muneharu, died the most ignominious death in the whole of the Korean campaign. After the fall of Chinju he was embraced by a courtesan called Nongae, who then flung herself backwards over the parapet of Chinju castle so that both fell to their deaths on the rocks below. In this print by Kuniyoshi we see him in a more flattering pose fighting against the Jurchens in Manchuria in 1592.

Kim Ch'ŏnil was watching from the top of one of Chinju's towers, and descended to the courtyard when he saw that the battle was lost. Accounts differ about how he died. One chronicler tells us that he 'bowed to the north, threw his weapons into the river, and killed himself beside the well at the foot of the tower.' Another states that he simply jumped into the river, as did many of the garrison, as noted by the chronicler of Katō Kiyomasa's exploits, which states that 'All the Chinese were terrified of our Japanese blades, and jumped into the river, but we pulled them out and cut off their heads.' Kikkawa's men on the far bank of the Nam River took a particularly active part in pulling escapees out of the river and beheading them. Some Japanese accounts note the taking of 20,000 heads at Chinju. Korean records claim 60,000 deaths, and both figures imply a massacre of soldiers and non-combatants alike.

That night, while the Nam River downstream from the castle walls flowed red and headless corpses still choked its banks, the victorious Japanese generals celebrated in the Ch'oksŏngnu Pavilion, from which the best view of this hellish scene could be appreciated. The *kisaeng* (courtesan) girls of Chinju were pressed into the service of the conquerors, and entertained them in the pavilion above the now ghastly river. That night one *kisaeng* struck a blow for Korea. A courtesan called Nongae became a target for the amorous affections of Keyamura Rokunosuke, a senior officer in the service of Katō Kiyomasa. Luring him close to the cliff edge, Nongae locked

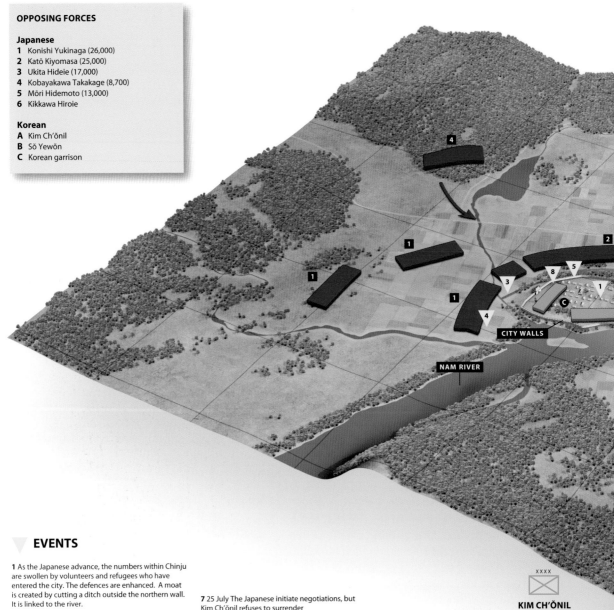

OPPOSING FORCES

Japanese
1 Konishi Yukinaga (26,000)
2 Katō Kiyomasa (25,000)
3 Ukita Hideie (17,000)
4 Kobayakawa Takakage (8,700)
5 Mōri Hidemoto (13,000)
6 Kikkawa Hiroie

Korean
A Kim Ch'ŏnil
B Sŏ Yewŏn
C Korean garrison

NAM RIVER

CITY WALLS

xxxx
KIM CH'ŎNIL

▼ EVENTS

1 As the Japanese advance, the numbers within Chinju are swollen by volunteers and refugees who have entered the city. The defences are enhanced. A moat is created by cutting a ditch outside the northern wall. It is linked to the river.

2 20 July: The Japanese arrive at Chinju and begin erecting siege lines. They are, however, determined that Chinju will fall quickly to avenge their previous disgrace.

3 21 July: The Japanese drain water from the new moat so that they can attack the northern walls.

4 22 July: The Japanese attack from the land side but the Koreans respond with great bravery. The Japanese attack is then temporarily halted.

5 23 July The Japanese erect static siege towers to allow them to observe Korean movements and to fire harquebuses into the city.

6 23 July: A volunteer army of Korean guerrillas approaches the city. This heartens the defenders, but the relief force is prevented from entering and is instead driven off by the Japanese.

7 25 July The Japanese initiate negotiations, but Kim Ch'ŏnil refuses to surrender

8 26 July: The Japanese under Katō Kiyomasa construct assault wagons to provide protection while the walls are undermined. These wagons are set on fire.

9 27 July: Katō Kiyomasa fireproofs more wagons and begins to undermine a section of the wall. A fortunate rainstorm leads to the wall's collapse

10 27 July afternoon: The walls are breached. Japanese troops enter and street fighting takes place. All Korean resistance quickly ends.

11 27 July, late afternoon: a massacre occurs of fleeing Koreans: soldiers and civilians alike. That night the Japanese commanders celebrate with Korean courtesans who have been pressed into service. One takes her revenge by pulling the general Keyamura Rokunosuke to his death in the river below.

THE SECOND SIEGE OF CHINJU, 1593

Ukita Hideie sacks the isolated fortress city in late July.

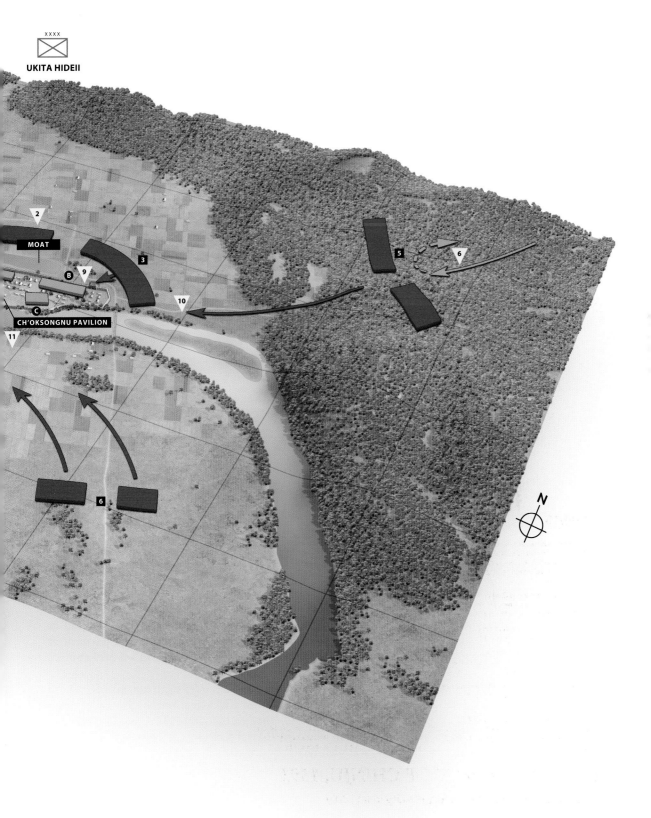

xxxx

UKITA HIDEII

2

MOAT

3

B   **9**

C

CH'OKSONGNU PAVILION

10

11

5

6

6

N

Nongae was the courtesan who pulled Keyamura Rokonusuke to his death after the siege of Chinju. In this bas-relief at Chinju she performs her heroic deed of self-sacrifice.

her arms into his passionate embrace of her, and flung herself suddenly backwards into the river, clinging on to her victim until both she and he were drowned. Nongae now has a memorial shrine next to the pavilion on Chinju's cliff, a heroine of the massacre of Chinju, Korea's worst military disaster of the entire Japanese campaign.

Yet, just like Pyŏkjeyek, the victory at Chinju changed nothing. Instead of following up their triumph with a counterattack against the advancing armies the Japanese retreated still farther. They were soon within the safety of Pusan which, together with the chain of coastal fortresses known as *wajō*, was to become the only occupied territory in Korea for the next four years. These tiny outposts of Japan remained as coastal enclaves until the second invasion began in 1597.

THE SECOND INVASION

THE SIEGE OF NAMWŎN

There was little military activity during the time of occupation. The invaders hung on to their coastal fortresses, but had almost no control over the rest of Korea, so the aim of the second invasion in 1597 was to put the matter right. Using the *wajō* as bases, a new army would land and advance on Seoul in an assault as rapid and as devastating as the blitzkrieg of 1592.

Unlike the 1592 offensive, the 1597 advance was conducted through the virgin territory of Chŏlla Province, from which Admiral Yi and the guerrillas had excluded the Japanese. It promised an alternative route to Seoul and fresh pickings for loot. The primary objective inside Chŏlla Province was its provincial capital Chŏnju, upon which two armies would converge. In overall command of the invasion was Kobayakawa Hideaki, heir of the late Kobayakawa Takakage. Ukita Hideie led the Army of the Left, while the former First Division of Konishi, Sō, Matsuura, Arima, Omura and Gotō were also present. Several other stalwarts of the first invasion such as Mōri Yoshinari and the Shimazu family made the total up to 49,600 men.

In the Army of the Right, of which 30,000 men supplied by Mōri Hidemoto made up nearly half the strength, the old Second and Third

The Japanese army lays down a barrage of harquebus fire against the walls of Namwŏn. From *Ehon Taikōki*, an illustrated life of Hideyoshi. The artist has tried to show the smooth-finished walls of Namwŏn that made climbing up so difficult.

The second invasion, 1597, and the liberation of Korea, 1598

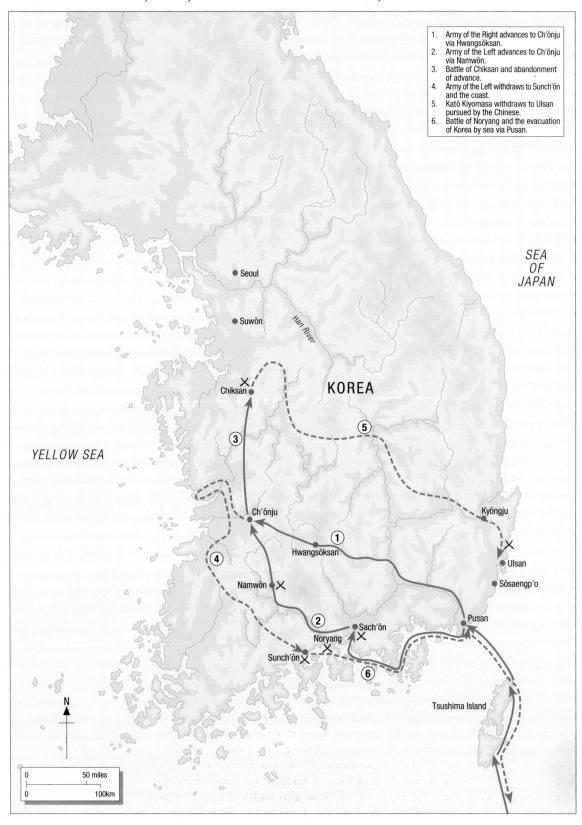

1. Army of the Right advances to Ch'ŏnju via Hwangsŏksan.
2. Army of the Left advances to Ch'ŏnju via Namwŏn.
3. Battle of Chiksan and abandonment of advance.
4. Army of the Left withdraws to Sunch'ŏn and the coast.
5. Katō Kiyomasa withdraws to Ulsan pursued by the Chinese.
6. Battle of Noryang and the evacuation of Korea by sea via Pusan.

divisions loomed large in the persons of Katō Kiyomasa, Nabeshima Naoshige (now accompanied by his son Katsushige) and Kuroda Nagamasa, all of whom brought extensive combat experience to a total of 64,300 troops. By this time the *wajō* garrison strength already in Korea was about 20,000, making the full Japanese army approximately 141,100 men, a number that is very similar to the 158,700 of 1592. The Army of the Right was to march directly north-west while the Army of the Left would be ferried round the now peaceful south coast to Sach'ŏn, where it would march towards the untouched fortress town of Namwŏn.

Namwŏn was a fortified town on a flat plain within encircling mountains, and therefore possessing none of the defensive features of the typical Korean *sansŏng*. To the south flowed a river, but this acted only as a distant moat. The town's layout was that of a rectangle of stone walls, pierced at the centre of each side by a gateway. Between each gate and corner the wall was built outwards in the form of a simple square-sided rectangular bastion to provide flanking fire on to the gates. The wall was about four metres high, almost vertical on the outside with a more pronounced slope inside. It was apparently plastered with shell-lime, and tiny fragments of shells made its surface glitter.

A few miles to the north, however, lay an alternative defensive position in the shape of the *sansŏng* of Kyŏryŏng. Erected about halfway up a high mountain, the fortress wall extended round the contours of the hillside in the typical serpentine model. The decision about where to make a stand was settled with the arrival in Namwŏn of the Ming general Yang Yuan at the head of 3,000 troops. The Korean garrison were for moving to Kyŏryŏng, where the Japanese would have had to attack uphill through wooded terrain, but Yang Yuan overruled them. He then began an extensive programme to strengthen Namwŏn's walls, adding another three metres to their height, and excavating a wide ditch six metres deep enclosed by a wooden palisade. Cannon were placed on top of the main gates and tree trunks were laid at the base of the ditch to slow down the attackers. A fortified reservoir to collect water was created outside the walls. Fences were also built out in the fields, but this tactic was to backfire when the Japanese used them as their own siege

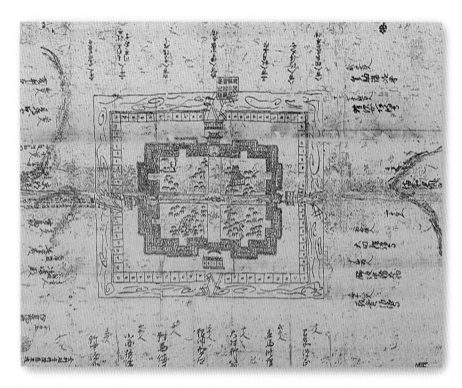

A contemporary Japanese map of the layout of Namwŏn, probably created to press a claim for reward. (Namwŏn Memorial Museum)

lines. The new defences had just been completed when the Japanese drew near on 22 September 1597 and, fearing lest the invaders should occupy Kyŏryŏng, Yang Yuan ordered its destruction.

The following day, as Japanese scouts began to appear, the defenders of Namwŏn were joined by Yi Pongnam, the military commander of Chŏlla Province, who arrived after much persuasion by Yang Yuan. There were now within the walls 6,000 defenders in total, split equally between Koreans and Chinese, together with almost as many civilians. On the attacking side Ukita Hideie took the southern sector, together with Wakizaka Yasuharu, Tōdō Takatora and Ota Kazuyoshi, while Konishi's old First Division covered the western side. Kurushima Michifusa and Katō Yoshiaki provided the contingent to the north, where they joined the Shimazu force, while 11 other generals prepared lines to the east. While the Japanese were still preparing their positions the defenders sallied out against them, but they were met by detachments of harquebusiers, and speedily withdrew. The following evening, as on so many occasions at the beginning of the first invasion, a delegation was sent to the defenders calling upon them to surrender and allow the Japanese a free passage through, and as on all those occasions this was again rejected.

A Japanese monk called Keinen, who accompanied Ota Kazuyoshi as his chaplain and wrote a diary, notes that it rained 'like a waterfall', turning the whole Japanese camp into a swamp. The following day he had his first sight of combat, which filled him with sadness. 'From along the whole line firearms and bows are being fired. One cannot but feel sympathy for those men who suffer death.' This happened on 23 September, when small detachments of Japanese harquebusiers targeted the defenders on the walls from the cover of the ruins of the houses they had destroyed or from the outer fences erected by Yang Yuan. The use of small group tactics meant that the Chinese cannon did little harm to the besiegers. The main body, in any case, stayed back well out of range.

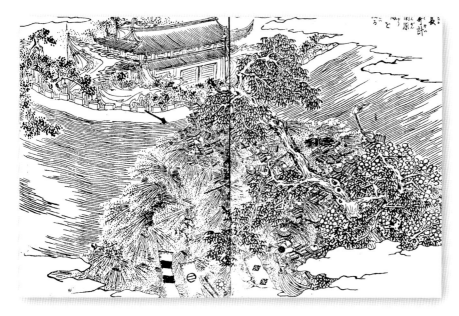

Namwŏn's defences were only breached when the Japanese piled up a huge number of bales of grass and rice to fill the moat and make an unsteady ramp. From here the samurai climbed into the city. From *Ehon Taikōki*, an illustrated life of Hideyoshi.

A very different view of the attack on Namwŏn comes from another follower of Ota Kazuyoshi, whose descriptions have a very different emphasis from those of Keinen. Okōchi Hidemoto's *Chōsen ki* (*Korean Chronicle*) was designed to glorify the exploits of his master, and also, quite plainly, Okōchi himself, because his personal role in the fighting is related with great prominence. Several other accounts exist, and all agree on one thing. The earlier rain cleared and was replaced by a fresh, bright moonlit night that was ideal for an assault. The attacks began at 10pm, when 'everything could be seen in minute detail' because of the bright moonlight, according to the Shimazu chronicler. The *Wakizaka ki* (*Chronicle of the Wakizaka family*) describes Wakizaka Yasuharu fighting on the southern wall alongside Tōdō Takatora:

> From within the castle great stones were thrown and fell like rain, and there were many wounded and dead. To add to this the stone walls were high and coated over with plaster, so they could not easily make their entry. His Lordship and Takatora had scaling ladders set up, and although one or two men fought over them, they succeeded in making their entry.

Meanwhile on the western wall Matsuura Shigenobu had secured an area of the ramparts and sent his standard-bearers in to raise the Matsuura flags on high from the walls. This would encourage the other attackers, and also inform them that the Matsuura troops had got there first.

The initial attack was driven off, and the Japanese were actually held at bay for another four days before a clever stratagem broke the stalemate. In preparation for the assault the Japanese foot soldiers scoured the nearby fields, cutting wild grass and the rice crop, which would otherwise soon have been harvested, and tying the stalks into large bundles, which were thrown into the moat at a chosen position. So many were collected that a huge and unsteady mound extended to the level of the ramparts. While harquebuses raked the walls with fire, a tactic aided by another bright moonlit night, bamboo scaling ladders were added to the pile ready for a determined assault. 'Around the evening of the day', writes Yu Sŏngnyong in *Chingbirok*, 'one could notice the soldiers guarding the ramparts of the fortress, whispering to

each other and preparing the saddles for their horse. It was apparent they
were anxious to escape.'

As the ramp neared completion fire arrows were loosed at the nearest
tower, and when this was set alight the samurai rushed on to the huge
heap of rice bales. Okōchi Hidemoto became the first to actually touch the
wall. He heaved his body on to the parapet while behind him swarmed
the Japanese footsoldiers, whom Okōchi refers to as 'our inferiors'. Okōchi
shouted for the flags to be brought up as quickly as possible, and dropped
down into Namwŏn, proclaiming his name like the samurai of old. Japanese
commanders' flags now flew triumphantly from various parts of the wall,
and numerous single combats began as the civilians huddled in their homes.
Okōchi killed two other men, and:

> Graciously calling to mind that this day was the fifteenth day of the eighth
> lunar month, the day dedicated to his tutelary *kami* [Hachiman] Dai Bosatsu,
> he put down his bloodstained blade and, pressing together his crimson-stained
> palms, bowed in veneration towards far off Japan. He cut off the noses and
> placed them inside a paper handkerchief, which he put into his armour.

Very soon the Japanese assault party were faced with a counterattack from
mounted men, yet even in all this confusion and danger the personal credit
for taking a head was all important:

> Okōchi cut at the right groin of the enemy on horseback and he tumbled
> down. As his groin was excruciatingly painful from this one assault he fell off
> on the left hand side. There were some samurai standing nearby and three of
> them struck at the mounted enemy to take his head. Four men had now cut
> him down, but as his plan of attack had been that the abdominal cut would
> make him fall off on the left, Okōchi came running round so that he would not
> be deprived of the head.

Nearby a bizarre encounter took place between a group of Japanese and a
giant Korean swordsman two metres in height. He was dressed in a black

suit of armour, and as he swung his long sword a samurai thrust his spear towards the man's armpit, only to catch his sleeve instead. At the same time another Japanese caught the man's other sleeve with his spear, ensuring that the warrior was now pinioned like a huge rod-operated puppet. He continued to swing his sword arm ineffectively from the elbow 'as if with the small arms of a woman', but the reduction of this once formidable foe drew only scorn from Okōchi. Impaled on two spears, and waving his arms pathetically, he reminded Okōchi of the statues of Deva kings in Buddhist temples with their muscular bodies and glaring eyes. With contempt and ridicule from his attackers the helpless giant was cut to pieces.

Soon Okōchi himself became a casualty. Attacked by a group of Koreans he was knocked to the ground, and as he was getting up several sword cuts were made to his chest, leaving him crouching and gasping for breath. His comrade Koike Shinhachirō came to his aid while Okōchi parried five sword strokes with the edge of his blade. A sixth slash struck home, cutting clean in two the middle finger of Okōchi's bow hand, but Okōchi still managed to rise to his feet and quickly decapitated his assailant.

Advancing more deeply into Namwŏn's alleys, Okōchi soon encountered another strong man dressed magnificently in a fine suit of armour on dark blue brocade. Okōchi was cut in four places on his sleeve armour, and received two arrow shafts that were fired deeply into his bow arm in two places, but in spite of these wounds he managed to overcome the man and take his head. Assuming that it belonged to a high-ranking warrior he took the trophy back to Ota Kazuyoshi. No one on the Japanese side was able to identify it, but after a short while it was shown to some Koreans who had been captured alive. They were taken aback, and as they looked at it in anger tears began to flow when they identified it as none other than the distinguished Kwangju magistrate Yi Chunwŏn. In the register of heads for the day this auspicious prize appears proudly next to the name of Okōchi Hidemoto.

Of the 3,726 heads counted that day, only Yi Chunwŏn's was kept intact. The others were discarded after the noses had been removed, the beginning of the process of nose collection in lieu of heads that was to become such a feature of the second invasion. Insisting upon proof of his soldiers' loyalty and achievements like the reward-giving generals of the ancient civil wars, Hideyoshi began to receive a steady stream of shipments of these ghastly trophies, pickled in salt and packed into wooden barrels, each one meticulously enumerated and recorded before leaving Korea. In Japan they were suitably interred in a mound near Hideyoshi's Great Buddha, and there they remain to this day inside Kyoto's least mentioned and most often avoided tourist attraction, the grassy burial mound that bears the erroneous name of the Mimizuka, the 'Mound of Ears'.

Eventually the city gates were opened by the defenders themselves as they sought to escape, but when they saw the massed ranks of the Japanese many simply bowed their heads to be decapitated, but a certain Kim Hyouei jumped into a rice paddy and pretended to be dead. He lay there until the Japanese

The pursuit after the fall of Namwŏn was a particularly terrible affair, with civilians being slaughtered along with fleeing soldiers. From *Ehon Taikōki*, an illustrated life of Hideyoshi.

withdrew and finally escaped. More killings followed when the troops of Katō Yoshiaki and Shimazu Yoshihiro, who were guarding the northern road, turned about to cut down any survivors fleeing in that direction. After a few hours of night fighting, when the moon and the white walls of Namwŏn both turned red from flames and blood, 'the torment was broken' to use the words of the monk Keinen. The civilian survivors were wailing bitterly as he walked in shock round the streets of the town, but worse scenes were to greet him over the next two days when he left the town 'and saw dead bodies lying near the road like grains of sand. My emotions were such that I could not even glance at them'. As he walked farther on he found more nose-less corpses in nearby houses, 'and this went on into the fields and mountains'. In the *Wakizaka ki*, however, the slaughter of civilians was just another phase in the military operation:

> From early dawn of the following morning we gave chase and hunted them in the mountains and scoured the villages for the distance of one day's travel. When they were cornered we made a wholesale slaughter of them. During a period of ten days we seized 10,000 of the enemy, but we did not cut off their heads. We cut off their noses, which told us how many heads there were. By this time Yasuharu's total of heads was over 2,000.

The bad news from Namwŏn travelled quickly northwards to the other Korean garrisons, and after just two days the Japanese Army of the Left marched out of Namwŏn to the provincial capital of Chŏnju and found it abandoned. The great prize of Chŏlla Province, the one piece of south Korean territory that had eluded them for the whole of the first invasion, was now securely in Japanese hands.

THE BATTLE OF CHIKSAN

The cataclysmic battle at Namwŏn, which is so well known and well recorded by both sides in the conflict, has completely overshadowed another successful battle fought by the Army of the Right the following day. This army was the larger of the two Japanese contingents. It faced resistance only from the *sansŏng* of Hwangsŏksan, an isolated mountain fortress that lay just east of the Chŏlla provincial border on top of a wooded hill. Its defenders had hastily recruited an army from the neighbouring districts, and many thousands of Korean troops were packed inside it. Katō Kiyomasa drew up his men to the south. Nabeshima Naoshige took the western station, while Kuroda Nagamasa covered the east. During the night of 27 September the Japanese took advantage of the moonlight that had aided the capture of Namwŏn the day before, and began a full-scale assault. The victory was as quick and as complete as that of Namwŏn, and 350 heads were taken.

There was no further opposition as the Army of the Right marched on to join their comrades in Chŏnju, but the threat to Seoul was becoming obvious to the Koreans, so a largely Ming force was hurriedly dispatched to halt their progress. The Chinese general advanced cautiously towards the town of Chiksan, where scouts informed him that the two armies were now but a short distance apart. Here he waited, and before long the Japanese force, which was under the overall command of Kuroda Nagamasa, also sent forward a vanguard unit. As dawn broke Nagamasa's vanguard reached a vantage point five kilometres north of Chiksan, from where they had a good view of what

appeared to be an immense Chinese horde below them. It was also obvious that the Chinese had seen them too, which placed the Japanese leadership in something of a quandary, because if they retreated the Chinese would pursue them and occupy the favourable ground that would allow them to fall upon Kuroda's troops. If the Japanese vanguard attacked they were likely to be annihilated, but in so doing they would slow the enemy advance and perhaps hold them down on the plain while Kuroda's main body followed. The crucial strategic objective appeared to be a rough earthen bridge across the river, to which the Chinese were heading. So, comparing themselves favourably to the 'forlorn hope' troops who had goaded Takeda Katsuyori into attacking at the famous battle of Nagashino in 1575, the Japanese advanced. On coming within range of the Chinese the foot soldiers opened up with their harquebuses, and the samurai attacked through the clouds of smoke.

The sound of firing reached Kuroda Nagamasa long before any of his messengers. A mounted unit under Gotō Mototsugu was sent directly forwards, while Kuroda rode out in support with the rest of his army as other messengers hastily galloped back to Mōri Hidemoto. When Gotō arrived on the higher ground he immediately comprehended the situation. The Japanese vanguard had advanced across the earthen bridge to engage the Chinese. They were now fighting with their backs to the river and were being slowly pushed back. The chronicler of the Kuroda family puts the following heroic words into Gotō's mouth, '… if the bridge is crossed by that great army then surely they will attack Nagamasa's main body …, so, accepting that only one man may be left alive for every ten that are killed, we must defend the bridge and prevent the enemy from crossing.'

Gotō therefore set off in a charge down the hill and led an advance across the river. The shock of the attack drove the immediate enemy back, and rallied the distressed Japanese. As soon as he was assured that the position

While a fierce hand-to-hand battle ensues outside, the defenders and their families in the burning fortress of Hwangsŏksan commit suicide. From *Ehon Taikōki*, an illustrated life of Hideyoshi.

A massive Ming army gathers to destroy the *wajō* of Ulsan, from a painted screen commissioned for the Nabeshima family, now owned by Saga Prefectural Museum.

had been reversed, Gotō withdrew his mounted force and returned to the high ground, where, according to the chronicler 'he came and went at various places, and gave the impression that the Japanese were a large force.' Very soon this impression became a reality when Kuroda Nagamasa appeared with the rest of his army. They quickly engaged the Chinese, whom they began to drive back until the Chinese were reinforced in their turn by 2,000 troops from Suwŏn. Once again the fierce fighting continued with no advantage to one side or the other, but then the final set of reinforcements arrived. These were Japanese, and consisted of Mōri Hidemoto's army. The arrival of their overwhelming numbers made the Ming army withdraw towards Suwŏn, but as it was now growing dark the Japanese command felt it imprudent to pursue them, so both armies disengaged.

This battle of Chiksan left the Japanese poised for a quick advance on Seoul and the achievement of Hideyoshi's war aims. But if Chiksan may have been an indecisive battle, it had decisive results. The post-Namwŏn panic that had seen Korean and Chinese armies abandoning positions had now been arrested, and it was clear that a large Chinese army was preparing to defend Seoul. Chiksan was therefore occupied by the Japanese to use as a base for the attack on the capital.

An advance on Seoul, and a re-run of their triumph in 1592, was therefore expected, but, just as at P'yŏngyang in 1592, the necessary troops never arrived and Chiksan was to become another last outpost of a Japanese advance. Seoul was never taken, and the reason why the attack never happened was again the result of a naval victory gained by Admiral Yi Sunsin at Myŏngyang. The 'miracle at Myŏngyang' as the Koreans called it prevented any movement of Japanese troops round the west coast of Korea through the Yellow Sea. With no reinforcements and a major Chinese advance another Japanese retreat was inevitable. It ended at the much-extended line of *wajō* that protected the coast. Three great sieges at Ulsan, Sunch'ŏn and Sach'ŏn followed, as described in my book Fortress 67: *Japanese Castles in Korea 1592–98* (Osprey Publishing Ltd: Oxford, 2007). All were Japanese victories, but each was completely nullified by the overall situation, which was that of covering the final evacuation to Japan and an end of the Korean invasion.

THE BATTLE OF NORYANG

The final trigger for the Japanese evacuation was the death of Toyotomi Hideyoshi. A withdrawal may have been inevitable anyway, but the commanders on the ground now had the freedom to act according to their own assessment of the situation. The Ming army on the eastern side of Korea, which was monitoring local movements after withdrawing to its base at Kyŏngju, became aware of troops moving out of Ulsan and Sŏsaengp'o and heading for Pusan. There was less movement over in the west because the allied navies were keeping Konishi Yukinaga confined to barracks in Sunch'ŏn, but the news of Hideyoshi's death finally leaked out to the ears of the Korean and Chinese. It was now certain that Konishi would attempt to escape, but the allied blockade was tight, so for the last time in the campaign Konishi Yukinaga turned to negotiations to ensure a safe passage. The Chinese admiral Chen Lin proved quite amenable to his advances, but Admiral Yi Sunsin would not agree to lift the blockade.

The Chinese had clearly had enough of war, and as Chen Lin was willing to let the Japanese go without further bloodshed, he proposed to Yi that he, Chen Lin, should conduct an operation against Sō Yoshitomo's small *wajō* on Namhae Island. Apart from the inherent promise of a final portion of military glory, Chen Lin also hoped that Konishi might take advantage of his absence and settle the matter by default by running the blockade. Yi, however, was greatly indignant at the suggestion of an attack on Namhae, which had long been within his sphere of influence. He knew that many Korean civilians were virtual prisoners of the Japanese there, and he feared that the Chinese would be unable to discriminate between them in a raid. Chen's subsequent and outrageous comment that any such Koreans should be regarded as collaborators who deserved to die anyway, confirmed Yi's worst suspicions about his ally and roused him to fury.

Nevertheless, the result of Konishi's determined pressure on the Chinese admiral ensured that one boat at least was able to escape from Sunch'ŏn. 'Yesterday two blockade captains ... chased a medium-sized Japanese vessel

The Noryang straits, between the island of Namhae and the mainland, were the site of the final battle of the Korean campaign, where Admiral Yi Sunsin was killed at the moment of victory.

fully loaded with provisions that was crossing the sea from Namhae', wrote Admiral Yi in what was to prove the last diary entry of his life. The ship was apprehended on its return, but a chain of signal fires then sent plumes of smoke from one *wajō* to another to inform Konishi that the message had succeeded in getting through. The troops stationed in Sach'ŏn, Kosŏng and Namhae quickly gathered at the agreed rendezvous point in the bay of Sach'ŏn, where they would be joined by Konishi for the voyage home. But when two days had passed and Konishi had not appeared, Shimazu realized that Konishi was still being prevented from leaving. The decision was therefore made to send 500 ships to Sunch'ŏn to run the blockade. The shortest route between the two bays was to head due west, and pass between Namhae Island and the Korean mainland through the narrow strait of Noryang.

Scouts and local fishermen informed Admiral Yi of what was happening. Anticipating that the Japanese fleet would take the direct route through the Noryang straits Yi drew up his fleet in the open sea just to the west of the narrow stretch of water. Late at night Yi was told that the Japanese fleet had sailed into the Noryang strait and was anchored for the night. It was the perfect opportunity for a surprise attack, which was launched at 2.00am on 17 December 1598. The battle, most of which took place in the narrow sea area that now lies under the Namhae suspension bridge, was conducted in perfect Korean style, and within hours almost half the Japanese fleet was either broken or burned. Admiral Yi was in the thick of the fighting, and personally wielded a bow when he rowed to the aid of Chen Lin, whose flagship came under attack from a group of Japanese ships. By the time the dawn was breaking the Japanese ships were retreating, and, sensing that this could be the last time for them to come to grips, Yi ordered a vigorous pursuit. It was at that moment, when victory was certain, that a Japanese sharpshooter put a bullet into Yi's left armpit. He was dead within minutes. Only three close associates saw the incident, and with his dying breath Yi asked them to keep his death a secret, so his body was covered with a shield and the battle of Noryang continued towards its victorious conclusion.

The death of Admiral Yi Sunsin, killed on board his flagship at the moment of his final victory like Nelson at Trafalgar, was a tragedy that deprived Korea of its ablest leader and greatest hero. Out of 500 Japanese ships only 50 survived to limp home. Shimazu Yoshihiro himself narrowly escaped death while other commanders provided protection from the Chinese ships that harassed them for a considerable distance.

There was only one act left to play in the drama of the Korean evacuation. Many Japanese soldiers and sailors had escaped to land on Namhae Island and took temporary refuge in Sō's now deserted *wajō*. The allied fleet burned any Japanese ships remaining in Noryang, so the survivors faced a long trudge across the mountains to its eastern coast. Five hundred of them were eventually rescued, probably by Konishi's fleet, which took advantage of the battle to slip out of Sunch'ŏn. They headed for Kŏje Island round the southern end of Namhae and docked at Pusan, Japan's last continental possession. Three days later the final evacuation began, and by the dying days of 1598, all the invaders had disembarked in Japan, where many heard for the first time the news that Hideyoshi was dead.

Back in Korea the Chinese and Korean forces began to enter and occupy the now deserted *wajō* of Ulsan, Sŏsaengpo, Sachŏn and Sunchŏn. Admiral Chen Lin even discovered some Japanese stragglers on Namhae Island who had not managed to make it to the eastern coast to be rescued by Konishi. They were all beheaded with great glee, and their heads taken to the Korean court as proof of the valuable role played by Korea's Chinese allies, but certain Korean officials suspected that in Chen's desire for a final glorious flourish, the Koreans on Namhae whom he had labelled collaborators had also been cut down, the tragic outcome that the late Admiral Yi Sunsin had so feared. It was a suitably sad ending to a long and terrible war.

BELOW LEFT
During the Korean campaign Katō Yoshiaki (1563-1631) was one of Hideyoshi's admirals, a position in which he had shown considerable aptitude in Hideyoshi's domestic wars. In this print by Kuniyoshi, however, he is shown standing on the battlements of one of the Japanese *wajō* forts.

BELOW RIGHT
A very good fibreglass replica of an ordinary Korean soldier at the Nagan Village Folk Museum near Sunch'ŏn. Unlike the Japanese foot soldiers Koreans wore no armour.

THE DEATH OF ADMIRAL YI AT THE NAVAL BATTLE OF NORYANG 1598 (pp. 88–89)

The battle of Noryang, fought in the straits that divide Namhae Island from the mainland, was the last battle of the Japanese invasion where the Korean navy gained a considerable victory over the Japanese fleet that was trying to escape. Tragically, at the height of the battle Admiral Yi Sunsin, Korea's greatest hero and the architect of so many naval victories, was hit by a bullet, and died on in the command tower of his ship as news was brought to him of his victory. To the rear of the plate the sea battle is at its height. As the Japanese army is evacuating Korea every ship has been pressed into action, even the lightly armed *kobaya* warship from which harquebuses are being discharged against the Korean fleet **(1)**. One of the famous Korean 'secret weapon' turtle ships is shown firing a cannon **(2)**. This is based on a reconstruction in the National War Museum in Seoul, which is now accepted as the most likely appearance of the legendary ship, even though there is still some controversy over whether or not the gun crews shared the same deck as the oarsmen.

The metal spikes on the upper deck discourage boarding. Admiral Yi is not on board a turtle ship but commands from an open-decked *p'anoksŏn* **(3)**. This has proved to be his undoing, because a Japanese bullet has hit him. Dropping his baton of command Yi falls. His shocked followers will conceal his body so that morale does not collapse. Yi is wearing a very fine general's armour of gold-plated metal scales over a heavy armoured coat. Beneath the armour is a heavy blue brocade robe **(4)**. All around him the fighting goes on. A drummer stirs the fighting spirit. Korean archers shelter behind tall wooden shields or the gunwales of the ship and keep up an arrow barrage against the Japanese. A bigger punch is packed by the iron cannon, which is lashed using rope to a wheeled gun carriage and is about to be discharged against the nearest Japanese ship **(5)**. The plate is based on drawings of the appearance of various Korean ships and an oil painting in the Memorial Shrine to Admiral Yi on the island of Hansando.

AFTERMATH

The samurai invasion of Korea was to have serious consequences for all three nations that took part in it, although on the Japanese side it was first hailed as a job well done. Okōchi Hidemoto provides the best example of the contemporary attitude to the Korean campaign when he concludes his *Chōsen ki* with a simple balance sheet. One hundred and sixty thousand Japanese troops had gone to Korea, where they had taken 185,738 Korean heads and 29,014 Chinese ones, a grand total of 214,752. The account had therefore ended in credit, in accordance with Hideyoshi's wishes. In a similar vein runs the account of Motoyama Yasumasa, who, like Okōchi, refers to the enduring monument to Japanese savagery that is the Mimizuka in Kyoto. Unlike Okōchi, however, the Motoyama account does not fail to mention that many of the noses interred therein were not of fighting soldiers but ordinary civilians, because 'Men and women, down to newborn infants, all were wiped out, none was left alive. Their noses were sliced off and pickled in salt.'

Of those who were not slaughtered, Keinen's diary had recorded the sight of Korean captives being led away in chains and bamboo collars by Japanese slave traders. Between 50,000 and 60,000 captives are believed to have been transported to Japan. Most were simple peasants, but there were also some men of learning and numerous craftsmen including medicine makers and gold smelters, but particularly well represented were the potters. The Japanese

Pusan Harbour was the first place at which the Japanese landed and the final one from which the peninsula was evacuated in 1598.

本朝英勇鏡
和藤内
三官

Katō Kiyomasa is shown here in this dramatic print wearing a *sashimono* flag bearing his *mon* (crest).

enthusiasm for the tea ceremony had ensured that at least one aspect of Korean culture was respected when the country was invaded, and it would certainly have astounded some anonymous Korean potter to hear that a simple peasant's rice bowl he had once made was doing service as a treasured and priceless tea vessel, handled by the greatest in the land. When the conquerors prepared to return home the opportunity to enrich their own pottery tradition at so little cost was too good to miss. The Shimazu brought 70 Koreans with them to Satsuma, including several potters who began ceramic production in three areas, and two centuries later visitors to Satsuma noted the distinctive Korean dress and language of the communities.

The political fallout from the invasion of Korea was not be realized in Japan for several years to come, although the invading armies returned to find Japan under the nominal rule of Hideyoshi's five-year-old son and on the brink of chaos. At the battle of Sekigahara in 1600 Tokugawa Ieyasu, the only prominent *daimyō* in Japan who had managed to avoid service in Korea, triumphed over a loose coalition to become shogun, a position his family was to occupy for the next two and a half centuries.

The war with Japan gravely weakened both Ming China and Korea, making the two countries easy prey for Nurhaci's Manchu invaders. The Ming collapsed in 1644 as a result of internal rebellions and a fateful decision to invite Manchu troops into China to crush the insurrection. The Koreans were closely allied to the Ming dynasty that had helped them so much against the Japanese, and when the Manchus invaded China Korea stood fast to its loyalty. Despairing of ever persuading the Koreans to change their allegiance, the Manchu Emperor invaded Korea and forced the king to flee to Kanghwa Island. The Korean king then pledged allegiance, and the Manchus withdrew. Once safely back in Seoul, however, the king repudiated his promise and began preparing for war. In January 1636 the Manchus invaded again, crossing the frozen Yalu River with 100,000 men. Their advance was so rapid that Kaesŏng fell within five days. The king sent the royal family to Kanghwa Island, intending to follow himself, but the Manchus cut the road and forced the king to flee south to the mountain fortress of Namhansansŏng. The castle was surrounded, and after a 45-day siege and with starvation looming the king surrendered. On Kanghwa the women of the court threw themselves into the sea to avoid capture, and in a brave gesture a loyal retainer took the ruling family's ancestral tablets into the pavilion over the south gate. Here he ignited a cache of gunpowder and blew everything to smithereens.

The Qing dynasty of China, created by the victorious Manchus, proved to be generous overlords and Korean independence was largely assured. For the next two centuries the 'Hermit Kingdom' of Korea stayed cut off from most of the known world, until the old regime was swept away with the coming of Europeans and the Sino-Japanese war at the end of the 19th century. During this conflict the modern Japanese army retraced many of the steps trodden by their ancestors, including a vicious battle for P'yŏngyang. The long Japanese occupation then stifled Korean aspirations towards self-government, even bringing about the re-writing of Korean history so that the samurai invasion of Korea became regarded as a heroic enterprise, rather than the savage act of aggression that it truly was.

THE BATTLEFIELDS TODAY

All the battlefields described here that lie within South Korea are easily accessible and worth visiting. In most cases there is a shrine and a museum commemorating the event. These have nearly all been built within the past 30 years because few original monuments survived the Japanese occupation of the 20th century or the devastation of the Korea War.

Travel within South Korea is easy and comfortable. A high-speed train runs between Seoul and Pusan. There are many motorways, and car hire is straightforward, but South Korea is one of the few countries that still requires an International Driving Permit in addition to the normal driving licence. I found long-distance buses to be convenient and very reasonably priced.

In Seoul two of the city gates have been restored, as have several of the ancient palaces, and the National War Memorial Museum is a good place to begin a study of the samurai invasion. North of Seoul the site of the battlefield of Pyŏkjeyek lies almost underneath a motorway, but memorials and a museum mark the site of the siege of Haengju, as befits a Korean victory. The topography of the hill is largely unchanged and there is a stunning view of the Han River.

In what is now an outer suburb of Pusan a fine shrine and memorials commemorate the defenders of Tongnae. Similar shrine complexes are to be found at Kŭmsan and Namwŏn, where the progress of the battles may be traced. The city of Chinju, with its fortress overlooking the river, is a very fine example. The sites and battles associated with the Japanese *wajō* castles are to be found in my book *Japanese Castles in Korea 1592–98* in the Osprey Fortress series.

Korean victories on land are therefore well memorialized, but even they do not compare with the degree of reverence and preservation that has gone into remembering the naval victories of Admiral Yi Sunsin. His statue seems to be everywhere, and every battlefield associated with him contains memorials and museums. All are located around the island-studded south coast, much of which is a National Park. The site of Yi's greatest victory at Hansando is suitably adorned. The island is reached by a ferry from the mainland, which takes one through the sea area where the battle of Hansando actually happened. On the island itself Yi's headquarters have been restored.

I have never visited North Korea, so have no information about the accessibility of sites associated with the Japanese invasion. However, I note from guidebooks and tourist information that visitors to P'yŏngyang are allowed to walk quite freely around the city. As the site of the siege now includes a park I assume it would not be difficult to trace its progress, but visitors must of course show great sensitivity, particularly in regard to anything that may be regarded as a military installation, so it is essential to check with the tour operator.

FURTHER READING

Yi Sunsin's reports and diary are translated in Ha, Tae-hung, *Nanjung Ilgi* (*The War Diaries of Admiral Yi*) (Seoul, 1977) and Ha, Tae-hung (trans.), & Lee, Chong-young (ed.), *Imjin Changch'o* (*Admiral Yi's Memorials to Court*) (Seoul, 1981). Yu Sŏngnyong's *Chingbirok* is now available in English translation as *The Book of Corrections: Reflections on the National Crisis during the Japanese Invasion of Korea 1592–1598*, translated by Choi Byonghyon (Berkeley, 2002).

A full account of the Korean invasions appears in my book *Samurai Invasion: Japan's Korean War 1592–1598* (London, 2002), where there is an extensive bibliography for Japanese sources and many more illustrations. Since that book was published, several important articles on the Korean campaign have been published. Kenneth Swope has made a particularly fine contribution because of his use of Chinese source material. See in particular 'Turning the Tide: The Strategic and Psychological Significance of the Liberation of P'yŏngyang in 1593' *War and Society* 21, (2003) pp. 1–22; and 'Crouching Tigers, Secret Weapons: Military Technology Employed During the Sino-Japanese–Korean War, 1592–1598' *The Journal of Military History* 69 (2005) pp. 11–41.